THE
GASLIGHTING
WORKBOOK
When Reality Isn't Real

**The Most Effective Methods to Avoid Mental Manipulation
and Trust Yourself Again After Psychological Abuse**

Dr. Theresa J. Covert

TABLE OF CONTENTS

INTRODUCTION
"QUARANTINED IN CLOUD-CUCKOO LAND"

You wouldn't be reading this book if someone wasn't causing problems for you, or maybe it's because you know a friend or family member who's suffering at the hands of another person. You may be feeling very confused, have tried to work out exactly what that person's doing and why, and you've just got to the point of exhaustion... Possibly, you're feeling guilty because you can't seem to control your life or your emotions. You may also feel yourself blazing with anger when you think of things that have been said and done to you - yet you're wondering what, if any of this, is your fault!

You are here because you believe you've been lied to or bullied and confused. And the other person denies everything. The problem is YOUR problem, they say - or imply. Apparently, you're living in "Cloud-Cuckoo Land," a ridiculously perfect world where you, and only you, think that things aren't as they should be. To add insult to injury, they won't even listen to you for a second, and you begin to feel that Cloud-Cuckoo Land has a locked gate! To keep you in... but why does a utopia need to shut you in?

This is a workbook to help people who've fallen victim to the technique known as GASLIGHTING. To explain it briefly: gaslighting is when someone tries to question, deny the truth of, ridicule, contradict, play games with, and just simply CONFUSE their victim. There are several reasons why some people employ this technique. Some use it to control to gain control over their victims; others use the victim to meet emotional, physical, or financial needs, or for vengeful purposes, or out of jealousy, or just for the fun of it.

Victims of gaslighting may be confused and frustrated, feeling ashamed of their reactions or wondering if they are going crazy, and it's all part of their imaginations. Is that you? Have you ever had the words "It's all in your head!" shouted at you before? Have you tried to get someone else to listen to your experiences, only to hear the same words?

Gaslighting can happen in different situations to people at any stage of life. Although we often think of it in marriages and intimate relationships, it can and does occur at work, or between people who are supposed to be friends; in families, at school, in the military forces, in shared accommodation - etcetera. Your colleagues can gaslight you or other colleagues; it could be your parents or the boss doing it to you. On the other hand, workers can do it to their employers, children to their parents. It can occur in group settings and public life. That last situation is somewhat different, and this workbook is mainly about one individual manipulating and confusing another. However, there are surprisingly common signs of gaslighting, wherever it happens, so it will still be relevant.

It doesn't matter if you find yourself in a position where you are being gaslighted, have been in such a position, or are new to this topic; this book has been written to help you see the truth and identify the signs. If it turns out that you're not being subjected to this type of manipulation, you will be able to accept that calmly and learn how not to be a victim of such an act in the future. If you are a victim, you will find helpful information and take yourself through several stages, reflecting on what you've learned. You'll recognize and understand gaslighting and start working on your life to become stronger, more focused, and happier within yourself. Once you achieve this, you can take control of your life again and be immune to further manipulation.

Once you start to see more clearly, you will breathe a sigh of relief!

Right at the beginning, let us start with an exercise. When you talk to someone about your problems, the first thing you do is to "get it all off your chest." Here, you can do that on paper so you can, with the guidance of the chapters and exercises you will go through, listen to yourself... and understand what's been going on.

EXPRESS YOURSELF BY BRAINSTORMING: AN EXERCISE TO START CLEARING YOUR MIND

To help you to understand what's been happening to you and going on around you, I'll start by getting you to do a BRAINSTORMING exercise. "Brainstorming" is when you speak or write every thought that comes to mind on a given topic. You don't censor it, or worry about what you come up with, or wonder what it all means, for now. Just get it all out and onto paper! If you prefer and can record your voice, you can just as easily talk to yourself about each topic.

You have a diagram for your guidance. There are two sections: one labeled "THE OTHER PERSON" and a second labeled "YOU."

The Other Person

What They Said

What They Did

What Others Said and Did

What Happened

You

What You Said

What You Did

What You Thought

How You Felt

1 In the first diagram, there are four topics where you will brainstorm about the person you think is manipulating or lying to you, gaslighting you, or whatever the truth may be, about things they have said and things they have done. Anything other people seem to be doing - to back up or agree with what that person says or does also goes in this section. Things that just happened and seem to be connected to that person go in here as well. I shall explain each one later.

2 In the second diagram, there are also four topics to brainstorm. These concern YOU. What have you said in your attempts to deal with this person? What have you done about the situation or to that person? Then, looking within yourself, ask yourself what you've been thinking during this time. Lastly, write about how you feel and have felt through it all.

! There's only one rule for guidance: try to keep to each topic. For example, if you're describing what you think about the other person's behavior, and you see yourself beginning to write about your feelings instead, then go to the part about how you feel and write it there. Or, if you're writing about what the person causing you trouble has done, and you move on to describe something you think they are responsible for but don't know for sure, rather put it under the heading, "What Happened."

So: eight headings. Under each one, just go for it! Get it out into the open as writing on a page or as a recording of yourself if you prefer. It's private: no one else has to see it. It's not once-and-for-all-time: if you wish, you can cross something out, or you can write it under another heading, as I've explained. Later, as you read the workbook, if you remember an incident or words or realize something, you can always add it.

TOPIC ONE: "WHAT DID HE/SHE SAY?"

Here, write about what the other person has SAID to you or what you've heard them say that has upset or confused you. Just write it down. Forget about whether or not you "should" feel the way you do about that person: we can look at that later. Focus on their actual WORDS. There is no order needed. If she told you, for example, that "You're trying to make our children love only you, and not me!", write those very words. If you need more space, then use a piece of paper or a file you can keep private on a computer, with the heading, "What Did He/She Say?" using 'he' or 'she' as appropriate.

TOPIC TWO: "WHAT DID HE/SHE DO?"

Under this heading, write as many of the deeds this person has done that made you feel abused, upset, or confused. Try to mention what he or she DID, not the words (because you have the first topic for those). For example, if he put an advertisement in the paper to sell the car you use, without even telling you, put that here. Use the space below, or as I've said, a page of paper or an electronic page.

TOPIC THREE: "WHAT DID OTHER PEOPLE SAY OR DO?"

Manipulative people often ask or entice a third party to "have a talk with you," do or say something to anger or confuse you, or try to make you feel guilty. These people are sometimes called "Flying Monkeys." Has anyone - apparently - been a "flying monkey" to you? Write down what they said and, or did. You may be unsure whether they were used deliberately to confuse or upset you, but it doesn't matter here.

If someone caused you grief in the subjects you think you're being gaslighted on, put it down here. Secondly, other people in your life may try to back up or re-enforce the actions and words of an abuser. This is unfortunate but true. They probably fall for the suggestion- and manipulation-tactics an abuser uses on them to make them perceive someone the way that abuser wants. So, for example, if you believe that your partner wants you to stop working outside the home, and thinks you are "not very capable," then when you apply for a really good job, family members may try to keep you 'in line,' doing the things you've always done: "But you've never worked so far from home before..." Write what they say or do.

TOPIC FOUR: "WHAT THINGS HAVE HAPPENED?"

Sometimes, when you're feeling very confused or suspicious about whether someone is manipulating you or lying, or maybe when you know that they've behaved to you with ill will but can't prove that they are responsible for some unpleasant incident or change in others... you can think you're going crazy. Don't worry about it now! What you can do here is write about what happened. It doesn't matter whether it will turn out to be caused by the person you think is gaslighting you or not.

If something happened that is suspicious, describe it. Just don't talk about your feelings (that is for later); stick to describing what you know to have happened. For example, Stooges always accepted your department's orders for flowers and herbs, and the store manager never queried these expenses, even though he is obsessed with trying to pay out as little money as possible for most things, and tells you (and others) that you spend too much. Suddenly, Stooges doesn't reply to your weekly e-mail order. You miss their delivery that week. When you phone them, they say that "Your store is a bit far away from our normal delivery rounds." That's odd: for two years, they've been delivering without complaint. Has the store manager said something to them? You don't really have a way to know. They are good people, but you don't feel that you could confront them or that it would be appropriate if you did. In that case, write down what actually happened: "Stooges didn't reply to my routine e-mail order, and didn't deliver anything that week. They told me it was because the store where I work is too far from their rounds. That has never been a problem before."

TOPIC FIVE: "WHAT HAVE I SAID?"

Looking at the second wheel in the diagram, now you can "brainstorm" about yourself. Firstly, what have you said to the person who you think may be trying to deceive or confuse you? Have you spoken to or confronted them? If other people are involved, what have you said to them? Once more, write down the actual words you used, as you remember them, or as near as you can remember.

You wouldn't write, "We had a fight about his staying out until three in the morning." Rather, you would write, "Why do you think you can just turn up at this time and not need to give any reason? Don't you know I was worried sick about you? I thought you'd had an accident" - if that was what you said. I don't mean to be harsh here: all I want is for you to channel these 'remembering exercises' into the right section, where you can tell it freely, just as it is or was!

TOPIC SIX: "WHAT HAVE I DONE?"

Here, talk about your actions regarding the situation. For example, if she went on and on saying that your dog is sick - when you couldn't see that it was - until eventually, you became so frustrated that you took it to the vet; then, write: "I took Fido to the vet to see if he's really sick or not. The vet found nothing wrong except an ingrowing claw."

Perhaps you are a woman who is suspicious that her husband is having an affair with his co-worker. You want some proof, and you find his diary when he's at work, and look for her name and number. You can write about your suspicions in the next topic, but here, just put: "I looked for his diary when he was away at work, found it and looked for Suzie's name and number. Her details are written there, but so are the names and numbers of all his other colleagues." That's really inconclusive, and your mind's spinning, but just stick to what you DID.

TOPIC SEVEN: "WHAT HAVE I BEEN THINKING ABOUT IT ALL?"

This part is where you have the freedom to speculate, to be open with yourself about your thoughts. Whether they are confused or not, don't worry! Just say what they are. All of this is private and personal. If you suspect something and somehow it doesn't seem rational, don't stop yourself from writing it down. It isn't a sin to examine your thoughts, and the time to judge the reality of them is yet to come. If you think, "He's trying to turn my family against me; but I don't know if that's why my aunt was so distant and a bit quiet when I went to see her the last time," then write: "I think that he's trying to turn my family against me." After that, write: "I think that my aunt was so awkward because he's said something unpleasant to her about me." You may find that your thoughts swing between positive and negative, believing something or doubting it: if that is so, don't panic! Just put down, for example: "Sometimes I think that thorn I found in my bicycle tire was pushed in deliberately: because it was so large if I'd ridden over it while cycling, I'd have had a flat tire while I was still on the way to college. On the other hand, sometimes I think of all those thorn-trees on the Farmstead Road and how often I got one in a tire, but it went flat slowly." You don't have to prove your thoughts here.

TOPIC EIGHT: "HOW DO I FEEL ABOUT IT ALL?"

This is the last heading, and it is extremely important. There is a tendency for men (who can also be victims of gaslighting) to avoid this topic and stay with what they thought or did. Women also, perhaps if you have a father figure whom you admire and whose rationality you idealize, may tend to think they are silly to focus on their feelings. It is true that some people put their feelings in the driving seat of their lives, so to speak, and lose control of them, become stressed and upset, fly into rages, confuse feeling with reality, and so on. Yet your inner senses and intuition are there for a reason, and you shouldn't ignore them. They may help you to sense what is to come, encourage you to avoid what is bad, and motivate you to keep holding on to what is good for you.

We can mention the "fact of your feelings" here. For example, someone is afraid of insects. She cringes at the thought of seeing her son's silkworms, let alone touching them... She does know that they're not poisonous, nor are the leaves they eat poisonous, nor can they bite you. Still, she feels repulsion. It is a fact that silkworms are not poisonous; however, it's also a fact that she is afraid of them. She isn't lying if she wrote, "I'm afraid of silkworms." Likewise, if someone says to herself, "I'm terrified that my husband and his lover are going to poison me," then whether or not they are plotting to do this, her fear needs to be acknowledged. Perhaps they WANT her to be afraid, and that fear alone is useful to them. So, if you want to clear your head, give yourself the freedom to describe your feelings. Your fears, your hopes, your desires, your doubts... Use emotion-words, such as "I'm angry; I'm confused but worn-out; I'm on a knife-edge; I'm in a rage and disappointed at the same time," or whatever you feel. Again, men especially need to be specific and not just use general headings. If you feel excited that someone's apologized but terrified that it might not be genuine, put "I'm excited but terrified at the same time."

CHAPTER 1:

YOU'RE NOT CRAZY: THEY'RE GASLIGHTING YOU!

"GASLIGHTING" is a word used to describe types of mental, emotional, and verbal abuse. It is a psychological effort to control and damage someone by denying the truth of their experiences and beliefs so that they become confused. Confused, unhappy people are easier to manipulate, and the gaslighter is someone who wants to make the victim dependent on him or her or use the victim to his or her advantage. The motives for this can be for plain self-interest, to get one or more of the good old "money, sex and power" goals, or as said before, to back up their feelings of superiority, or to take revenge.

Quite simply, it is a hidden attempt to make you think that you're crazy, forgetful, unable to handle any challenge, or take any responsibility! The word came from a stage-play by British playwright Patrick Hamilton, which saw its first performance in 1938, called "Gas Light." It was made into a film twice: in 1940 in Britain, and in 1944 in the USA.

Every victim has a story. This is the basic story of "Gas Light": in London in 1880, Jack and Bella Manningham live in an upper-middle-class apartment. He is a bully and openly flirts with their two female servants - whereas Bella seems to be neurotic and stressed. Jack started going away in the evening and will not tell his wife where he goes or why. While she is alone (and always while she's alone), she thinks she hears footsteps in the empty apartment above and that the old gas-powered lights in their home are going dim. The apartment above was lived in by Alice Barlow, a wealthy woman who died. Jack tries to convince Bella that she imagines the noises, that the gas lights are perfectly all right, and that it is all 'in her head.' At the time the play begins, his machinations have already been successful, and Bella is confused.

However, when a police detective appears and tells Bella that he is investigating the unsolved murder of Alice Barlow and that the motive seems to have been to steal her valuable jewelry, Bella begins to realize the truth: Jack is letting himself into the empty flat and walking around, trying to find where Alice hid her valuables. He has the lights up there burning on full to aid his search... and this makes the piped gas-pressure drop in their apartment, thus causing the light to dim. Bella is persuaded to help the police to expose Jack, which she does, but she takes revenge by pretending to help him to escape. She says to him ironically that because she is "insane," she cannot be held responsible for her actions... Jack is, of course, arrested.

The story was considered to be successful and has been acted, adapted, and filmed many times. It has, of course, given its name to the attempt to give false information to confuse and manipulate someone. Yet, among the many good reviews this play or film has had over the years, one often reads critics who think it is somehow silly and unbelievable, that Bella is weak-minded or unintelligent, or the story's outdated, limited to the Victorian era in which it is set. Well, dear reader, the psychological and counseling professions do NOT agree... Patrick Hamilton's skill in staging this thriller makes it work well, but only as much as his understanding of human nature!

So what kind of things do gaslighters do to their victims? We have this example, but gaslighting is a wide-ranging problem in abusive relationships. It is time to examine it more closely.

The gaslighter may be an openly arrogant or difficult individual or a quiet type. What is common to both extremes is the attempt to make you doubt yourself, your reasoning, and your memory in a hidden way so that you don't notice what is being done and its effects. You may hear a lie from this person that sounds so odd that it makes you question your memory... or your recall of events may be rejected, mocked, and ridiculed outright. In either way, it makes you go back again and again to your memory, which is a sort of circular action. Because as you repeat this, you may end up wondering if you've modified your original impression of what happened, that perhaps you remember your last memory exercise and not the actual event. There you are! Now you are in doubt.

The degree of gaslighting can also vary. Not every abuser wants you to be sent to a mental hospital, commit suicide, or be 'framed' for murder! While these things have occasionally happened from gaslighting techniques, much more often, the gaslighter wants to keep some kind of control over you, even just stage a sort of repeated 'play' where he or she gets to look good, gets sympathy from others, or can make himself or herself look like a helping "angel" to your weaknesses - while actually worsening them secretly. The whole point is to get something to their advantage: if it really is in their best interest to have you banging on the walls of a padded cell, they'll try to get you there. However, if you're far more useful as a sort of glorified servant in the home, to give an illustration, they'll just want to make you do so badly at your job that you resign or get fired.

Another tactic is when the abuser asks questions publicly, to which you know he or she has the answer. It's feigned ignorance. Here is an example: I mean, if the boss told you to plot out the dividing line at thirty-one meters, ninety-eight feet, or whatever, and later on there's a site-meeting with the neighbors, why does he ask you, "How far is this boundary from the next property?" Probably because the neighbor is expecting to hear you say thirty meters, and when you say thirty-one, it makes you look incompetent! Or else, if the neighbor doesn't protest, your boss knows that he's just helped himself to one meter, three feet approximately, of his neighbor's property! When he keeps on and on asking you later - and getting other people to ask you - what the measurement was, where the next line is, how far the opposite wall is going to be, etc., etc. until you say that you'll need to get out the plans because you don't have a photographic memory, you are being made to doubt your recall that it was HE who told you to put that line at thirty-one meters... He's gaslighting you, and in this case, your neighbor as well. This and other like-minded tactics use what is called 'innuendo,' a subtle hint or shade of meaning.

Lying goes with the gaslighter's job. Sometimes it is subtle, but just as often, it is blatant and compulsive. The compulsive, grandiose, narcissistic liar tells a lie and then denies it with another. He or she tells so many that you wonder how they remember them all: in my opinion, they actually don't! They just keep a very good watch on WHAT situation they are lying about and what they want out of it. Amid the tangled masses of lies and just as many counter-accusations, other people, especially the principal victim or victims, become confused because they are trying to remember all the different lies, answer all the accusations, and may not know what the liar wants out of the situation.

Denial is an important element of gaslighting. The words "I never said that," "You didn't do that," and "It wasn't as much as that" are used a lot by a gaslighter. This denial ranges from very subtle, e.g., "That hundred dollars - ninety, actually - was meant for..." to an open, arrogant, hybris-fuelled denial with the evidence in plain view! "Of course, I didn't steal that watch!"
"But it's in your handbag!"
"Someone's put it there."
"Who? There was no one else in the shop."
"You don't know that! Someone could've crept through the door. It was planted on me!"
"That's impossible! Who's trying to put watches in your handbag? Other than you..."
"How dare you! I've been set up, and you don't even stand up for me!!"

Counter-accusations are an essential strategy in gaslighting. They are a sort of mirror-image of the truth, and since someone who is gaslighting another person is an individual who wants you to question YOUR view of reality, it helps to have a pre-digested, easily understood alternative at hand. If you are struggling to concentrate, or if you experience any kind of fear of your gaslighter and are being threatened, your mind can feel an urge to give up and accept this alternative. Maybe your abuser will accuse YOU of gaslighting THEM... In a different way, the alternative can be used suddenly as a distraction from the real issue. For example, if a woman thought her husband was having an affair and said that she found incriminating texts on his phone; if he has a gaslighting type of personality, he may strike back verbally by accusing her of having texts from another man on HER phone! He might demand that she produce hers, go through it, and jump on the first one he sees (even if it turns out to be from the plumber) and accuse her of having an affair. It might be an excuse for him to start following her around or trying to restrict her movements. He may repeat the counter-accusation so many times that she starts feeling guilty for contacting the plumber and deletes his number from her list of contacts. Her husband may demand to see her phone again, look at the contacts, and find out that the name is gone - and he will use this as 'proof' that his wife was indeed having an affair. In all of this, a counter-accusation serves to take her attention away from the matter which started the dispute: the fact of there being personal texts on the HUSBAND'S telephone!

Another truth-twisting move also involves two opposites: a gaslighting personality may behave in two diametrically-opposite ways on two days in succession, for example here: on one day she may burst into theatrical tears and accuse her boyfriend of being tied to his mother's apron strings, selfish with regard to the things he talks to her about, mean with money for the things they need in the house - and no good in bed...! He goes to work a night shift in a rage but is deeply hurt. When he returns, she'll greet him lovingly and inquire about his day as if nothing had happened!! The fact that he feels pressured into returning the greeting with a pleasant answer since he's exhausted and in no mood to have another argument is something she will take as a successful attempt at manipulation. She will tell herself that she can make him argue and hurt him when she wants; she can make him tame and polite whenever she wants and shut down his attempts to answer back. If he did try to express his anger with her previous behavior, she will act as if hurt and wounded that her seemingly pleasant words were answered with criticism. This kind of behavior, over time, will confuse the victim considerably.

The techniques, tricks, and plots of gaslighting are, unfortunately, very complex if you try to classify all the possible ones. They are as complicated as human nature. However, most of them do fall into several easy-to-identify types, which I've gone through. To recap:

 Gaslighting can be anywhere from OPEN hostility and confusion-tactics to SUBTLE sabotage that happens under a friendly or neutral-looking sort of mask, and anywhere in between.

The deception could be an attempt to DESTROY you; or maybe only to BOTHER you, e.g., make you feel guilty - or some agenda in-between, to USE you thoroughly.

 Gaslighting often uses subtle hints, distortions, and suggestions, called INNUENDO.

LYING is part of all gaslighting, but it can be anything from blatant and childish to slight and sneaky.

 DENIAL is a common response of gaslighters to any attempt to correct facts or accuse them: from screamed words to nonchalant, shrugging-off gestures and the frequent use of the word, "No".

A gaslighter uses COUNTER-ACCUSATION as an attempt to take attention away from any interrogation of his or her deeds. It may be an accusation of a different trespass, but more often, it's an open reversal, making you feel guilty of exactly what they are guilty of.

 Another type of confusion-strategy is to behave in two opposite ways in quick succession, in other words, to be TWO-FACED. It's denial in manners more than in words.

EXERCISES TO FOCUS YOU

I want you to look now at the exercises you wrote under the circle titled "THE OTHER PERSON." If you want to be more certain about what might be happening to you, then try to answer these questions:

INNUENDO

Answer this question "What examples, if any, can you think of which are innuendo: hints, unpleasant twisting of facts, in the actual words of that person?" under the topics of "What Other People Did or Said," and "What He or She Said."

_____

_____

_____

_____

_____

_____

LYING!

Read what you wrote about "What He or She Said." What is there that is a definite lie? You can make a connection with some arrows, or put a)s, b)s, c)s, etc., in the topic "What He or She Did" or to "What Happened" when one refers to the other.

_____

_____

_____

_____

DENIAL

You can do exactly the same here with the subject of denial. List that person's denials, and link them to things that they did or that happened. You can also look at the circle called "YOU" and read what you said to them. Don't be too worried here about the truth or otherwise of what you accused them of. I'm not saying and don't mean that such is not important; just focus for now on what they denied and in what words.

✒

_____

_____

_____

_____

_____

COUNTER - ACCUSATION

Have you been accused of something which was the very thing you felt was being done by the person doing the accusing? Or have they made accusations against you which are of some other kind, but which seem to be a smoke-screen to deflect your awareness of what THEY are getting up to? Write down as accurately as you can what you were accused of.

✒

_____

_____

_____

_____

_____

CHAPTER 2:

GASLIGHTING AND CHILDHOOD

In this chapter, I will show you how your childhood experiences can make you vulnerable to an abusive person and sensitive to their efforts to gaslight you. Please note: I'm not accusing you automatically beforehand of having had an unhappy childhood; maybe yours wasn't so bad. Gaslighters can try their tactics on anyone and everyone, especially in an organization or a group. However, what is really important to understand is that your own personal 'woundedness' and experience of trauma in childhood, if you've suffered significantly, will indeed make you susceptible to the tactics of any narcissistic, manipulative individual. Such people are also fairly good at identifying potential victims.

This may be an unpleasant but necessary truth for you to hear. Therefore, in this chapter, it's time to have a look at your earliest years, but take heart: if your inner wounds make you become a victim of a gaslighter more easily and to a greater degree, then as you begin to understand your emotions and memories, and heal from the damage even years after it was done to you, then you'll become a lot less vulnerable! Less-impressionable people resist the efforts to fool or confuse them better and more easily. A would-be gaslighter is also less likely to bother trying if he or she sees that you don't respond!!

Most people get their first ideas and impressions of love and personal bonds from how their parents interact with one another. All that is just as it should be, except that when the parents are abusive to each other, have serious personal problems in their treatment of people generally, or when one abuses, or both gang up to abuse their child or children, the child develops a warped idea of what intimate relationships are. Such a child will find it hard to love or be loved. I'm sure you've had to bear with living or staying next to, or near, a certain family where everyone screams at each other several times a day... if there are children in that family, imagine how that will affect their views on love and life in general?

One thing is clear: anyone who gaslights someone else - deliberately distorting the truth for them, trying to influence them by causing them mental distress and damage - is some sort of sociopath. It's a bit obvious, isn't it? Psychologists call some of them 'anti-social personalities,' or they can be 'covert narcissists.' Anti-socials basically couldn't care about anyone or anything and may use gaslighting to get what they want from you if that's just a way to get it faster. Covert narcissists are worse in that they are aware of their narcissistic self-love, yet they hide it, knowing that they'll get more out of people if they project some sort of lovable, at least average-looking, seemingly caring personality.

They put on a mask, and it can be very effective. Yet underneath, they have chosen not to feel for and care about anyone else. Those who get to know them would come to see this, and in order to continue their parasitic use of others, such covert narcissists often try to control their victims with delusions, lies, and confusion-tactics.

Some people have genuine difficulty trying to "stand in the shoes" of others and may, perhaps unjustly, be labeled as "anti-social." But there are others who can see and understand you well enough (creepily well enough, sometimes!) and use your weaknesses to control you, even fool and use those around you, all without caring even slightly about YOU or others. Not good...

If you are abused emotionally (or physically - you can't separate them here) by a parent or caregiver (to use a broader term) when you are very young, there's almost no way to survive it except by sort of 'giving in' and accepting their view of you and the world! People who look at the attachment of children to abusive caregivers compare it to the behavior of a puppy in a pack of dogs. Puppies can't FIGHT the adults (including their mother and their sire/father) who are fully grown; they can't run away because FLIGHT would lead them into a hostile world, all alone and inexperienced. Puppies can FREEZE with fear when an adult intimidates them (puts its teeth to the puppy's neck), but they can't live like that all the time, so they FAWN. They try to make everyone love them, try to adore all the adults, rush up and beg for attention... and even when rejected, they just try again... and again.

For a human child with human reasoning, fawning implies that you accepted a whole lot of false ideas about yourself and your abuser. What kind of false ideas? Let me give you some examples: you are lovable only when you shut up and make yourself 'invisible'; you are lovable only when you do well at school; you are lovable only when you never complain about your brother, who's allowed to do what he wants first because he's older... Do you see? Love in these cases is conditional; you have to put on an act to get it, possibly hiding your real emotions, but worse than that, actually believing that when you feel admiration and tolerance for the people who display such behavior, you are doing good!

Neglect in childhood is another type of trauma that will affect you in later life. I don't have to mean that you were locked in a dark room for days with nothing but a loaf of bread and a pitcher of water... just that children need time and attention to mature, learn and grow.

If a child is ignored most of the time - maybe punished for seeking attention, and praised for sitting quietly, daydreaming and amusing herself, or when she rushes to wash the dishes after the meal - she learns that it is wrong for her to have any of her own needs met. She will grow up as a helpful, undemanding, empathetic person - but one who doesn't know how to look after herself. I'm hardly suggesting that children shouldn't help you to wash the dishes: no, the difference between a well-brought-up child and a neglected one is that the neglected child gets no interest in herself at all. A loving caregiver can tell a child to help with the dishes, and while they work together, the child interacts with the caregiver, learning about things and talking about herself or himself. The neglected child is like a servant in the house, present as a silent spectator while the "employers" go about their own business which is usually nothing to do with him or her, yet nevertheless, they expect him or her (this is a horrible little detail and important) to 'pick up,' hear, understand and remember any event or action that is of concern to that "servant." Literally, the servant (in this case, the child) must be able to read their minds!

Inside an abused, crushed, punished, hated, or ignored child is a lot of shame and a desire for love (it's what we're made for) that has been thwarted. An ignored child such as the one I mentioned has grown up seeing that people have company. In an abusive or narcissistic family (abuse isn't only committed by one person, to one other...), that company is not shared with the child, who in this case is the victim. We are made for human company, and so he or she will feel a deep, inner loneliness, a longing to have at least what their caregivers had. Tragically, that might have been a very conflicted, stressful relationship, but at least it wasn't loneliness. All of this makes the victim hunger for relationships or attachments desperately in adult life, and any old company, any old relationship, will do, so to say.

Why do such children not learn from their abusers and warped role models to become abusers/narcissists themselves? The brutal truth is that some do. However, I believe that there is an inner choice some people make, usually in childhood, namely: TO TRY TO LOVE IN ORDER TO GET LOVE. It's only human, and it's done out of ignorance of true love - I mean, we are talking about children who know little about the world as yet - and in a way, it works. The fawning puppy gets some attention, food, and protection and lives another day. It is terribly insecure and unable to protect itself, unfortunately. That is no problem when you are a puppy, to use this analogy of dogs. After all, puppies grow up and learn to do what dogs do: fight (even play-fight), co-operate, assert themselves, submit to the pack leader, find a mate, and have their own puppies.

Human fawners get stuck with their childhood idea of love, growing up physically and intellectually, but not emotionally and spiritually. In this harsh world, they are 'honey' for the 'honey badgers' looking for easy victims.

The opposite inner choice is the one that gives birth to an abuser: TO TRY TO GET POWER IN ORDER TO GET LOVE. They feel the effects of others having power over them, and in their childish helplessness, they start to wish they could have that power to give them the attention and the things they want. One way is they begin to hide information from their caregivers, to hide their own feelings of fear and weakness, or to exploit their caregiver's weaknesses. Or maybe they learn to become actors: so they can be loved conditionally, they appear to do what will get them attention, without actually meaning it. We often lie as children: these ones decide (and start to prove in an abusive family) that lying to survive works better than the truth. For example, if a child is the elder brother who always gets preference over his baby brother, for the little attention a parent gives grudgingly, he learns that he is more entitled to attention. The power and knowledge of his extra years give him the advantage over his baby brother. As an adult, will such an individual not seek to get love from someone he or she uses as a pawn, a slave? To get "love" by force - or craft, by lying and deception? The use of craft and deception brings us to the character of a gaslighter.

You can see that there is a moral choice at the heart of this. Dear reader, if "loving to get love" was the choice you made as a suffering child - I admire you! It was the right choice at the time. However, I can't judge the one who chose "to love to survive" because you didn't have a true, healthy, adult morality; couldn't have. It wasn't your fault. The key to growing and healing from the abuse of a gaslighter, and your own unhappy childhood, is to learn to love wisely. That means being able to love yourself and respect others while protecting your own boundaries. Some victims literally cry, "but I'm trying to be good, I'm trying to do my duty!" Their morality is fake in some ways. It needs to grow up with them. Self-hate and shame are not love and don't actually help you to love others. When you can love your neighbor as yourself, not love your neighbor and hate yourself, you will be so much happier! You will also be more, not less, loving.

So, a good child decides and learns to be the child a selfish, manipulative parent will like, escaping the coldness, violence, anger, and punishments he or she would get otherwise. It's a survival strategy. Though some victims manage to grow out of this mindset by the time they are adults, many do not. Their abusive caregiver of childhood continues to manipulate them and control what they do for years and years.

That's bad enough, but the added crime is that an abused child becomes an easy target for other abusers. Someone who's been taught that love is made out of appeasing difficult, capricious people and trying hard to get tiny scraps of attention from them will look useful to difficult, capricious, selfish, abusive individuals. The strain and drama of their childhood are so familiar that when they experience something similar again as an adult in new intimate relationships - or any kind of relationship in business, social life, and so on - they can even feel loved, or that there is a need for them to be loving. It looks to be a purpose in life for them, the pitiful servants they feel themselves to be. A narcissist is a person who doesn't really want to be intimate with anyone but wants to be surrounded by "servants" who can be ordered about or tricked and manipulated to do the bidding of that "Narc" (the abbreviation of the word "Narcissist"). "Servant looking for a position in a household," says your attitude and behavior; if you are deficient in self-respect and self-love and have decided, all the same, to love in order to get love. Such servants can and do find willing employers who start to damage and destroy them from within. You may not realize this, but deep inside, a narcissistic personality is a fear of being abandoned (oddly, very similar to yours if you are traumatized) and not getting attention or not being liked. They are frantic to be liked, in their case, because they think they deserve to be liked far more than anyone else... and someone who could see into them and not like what they see is hardly going to be of much use. You come along with a desperate desire to like other people, trying hard because you think you deserve to be liked less than most people do... and, bang! Opposites attract.

"Narcs" are people who are good at picking out victims and look for them actively. People who may not be quite as malicious, but still have hidden agendas, will be able to judge that someone is a suitable target when and as they come across one who is. You might be asking what this has to do with gaslighting, which is the specific topic of this workbook. The truth you need to understand is that if you were forced to be a "good child," you learned to give up your own desires, sacrifice your ability to make decisions; basically, you had to SURRENDER YOUR OWN REALITY. You had to accept someone else's will and view of the world... does that sound familiar? That's what happens to you later on when you're being GASLIGHTED!!

You may not be able to remember all of the pain and insecurity of your childhood. That isn't to say that you've forgotten everything, blanked out the whole lot - but it is very likely that you have pushed some of the worst memories, the memories of how you FELT, deep down in yourself. You did it to cope, but those wounds still hurt!

A professional counselor or psychologist, who has experience of helping people who have been abused and confused, can do more than you can on willpower alone. I am giving you the condensed advice of other people, and it is an objective, outside source of help to you. Don't stop there: get as much objective outside help as you can!

Nothing about what I've shared and written suggests that there are more girls than boys who are manipulated and distorted in childhood. Nothing I've explained would justify thinking that fewer boys than girls decide to fawn and to love with the love of a servant. So, if you are a man reading this, and you can see that you've been gaslighted, that you were ill-treated in childhood, leading to a desire to give a love born out of your feelings of shame and unworthiness... you picked the right book!!

You are not alone. The world is full of crushed husbands and dutiful, depressed sons. It can be that your same-sex parent or caregiver abused you emotionally, or perhaps it was your opposite-sex parent. Don't think of your inner weakness as a sign that you are not sufficiently male: the crushed inner child of any victim can be a boy or a girl. When you start to heal and to confront the lies stored away within you, your masculine maturity, if you are male, or your feminine maturity, if you are female, will give you inner peace. You will be able to love with an adult love of whatever kind you were meant to have!

Some of your bad memories of a controlling parent are remembered more as FEELINGS than as scenes and stories. If you've been in an abusive relationship or personal situation recently or are still in one, ask yourself if some of the physical sensations you get are sensations you can remember when you were little.

Do you start to shake and stutter when you're being shouted at or becoming confused, for example? Did you use to do that when you were small? Think about it, and there will be a place for your answer in the exercises to come...

Here is a fictional story to illustrate emotional abuse in childhood, that made its victim to be found by an abuser and gaslighted in adulthood:

Lucetta came from a family with many aunts and uncles, but she was an only child. The family members were close to each other, but because they were immigrants in a town with few other residents from their country, they tended to isolate themselves. Lucetta was often left alone and brought up very strictly, always to do as she was told. Her mother and father rewarded her when she was quiet and uncomplaining and punished swiftly if she ever tried to talk back. She was known as "a good girl," and she knew that this meant she was expected to agree with them at all times! In her family, the company of other children was discouraged, and Lucetta had to go home straight after school, supposedly because these other children would bully her.

Lucetta was mature in some ways; she was expected to talk to and experienced in talking to adults about their concerns. She was a hard worker at home, doing household chores to serve others, especially her mother, who was a hypochondriac. She was expected to sympathize with her mother and never be sick herself. Her father accepted this, being very detached from his daughter and preferring that Lucetta, not him, listened to his wife's tales of sickness. He didn't have any reluctance in ordering her around, though. After school, Lucetta was never sent to college because she was told by her parents she was 'not the intellectual type' though her teachers disagreed, for her marks were good.

At the age of twenty, Lucetta met Dave at the grocery store. She was quiet and polite; he, talkative but insecure. Her family didn't approve of her staying out talking to Dave after his work-shifts ended, but they didn't actually disagree with the idea of her marrying him, as his father was born in their country, and they imagined a married Lucetta living down the road from them and coming by every day to check on her mother. Lucetta fell in love totally with Dave, and Dave didn't waste any time preparing for their marriage, which happened soon after she turned twenty-one. The honeymoon was soon over: Lucetta realized that Dave was insecure, obsessive, and needed to be felt sorry for all the time, talking endlessly about his hopes and plans. He was also very mean with money.

Lucetta ended up like a rope in a tug-of-war: her mother would cry and shout because her daughter didn't spend as much time listening to or helping her in the family home as before - and Dave resented her going there because he had his ideas and needed someone to tell them to. She became stressed and felt guilty. Dave was beginning to dislike Lucetta's family a lot and one day announced that he'd got a job in another state, at a different branch of the same grocery store, and that they were moving. Lucetta half-wanted to move because she realized how her mother used her for sympathy, but she still felt guilty.

In their new city, it was necessary for Lucetta to get work, for them to manage. She became a shop assistant and, though shy, started to like it. People liked her... Dave didn't seem impressed, though, and kept asking her if she wasn't overdoing it... It was true that she stressed herself about not being nearer to her own family, and Dave wasn't keen on her going to see them more than once a month. She could sort of see that, and it did cost money: but she asked herself why Dave seemed to resent her job. Every time she was tired, made a mistake, or had to put off doing something, he would say: "You're not coping. You should give up that job." This didn't stop Dave from calling her at work to tell her about things or talking for hours about his plans to set up his own business.

Dave began complaining that Lucetta wasn't cooking properly anymore and that worrying about her own family was making her sick. He corrected her all the time and said that she was losing her memory. She'd sometimes protest that she had remembered an incident, but doing so would make him very angry, and she found it easier to give in and accept his version. Dave's few acquaintances at work seemed to think that he was a kind of martyr who had to look after a sick wife. She felt half-angry upon hearing this, yet so guilty about herself that she half-wondered if it was true. He told her again and again that she should give up her job and began to pester her to see a doctor, that her hands were shaking, and so on. Eventually, her performance at work suffered, and reluctantly she gave up her job. It seemed to make Dave happier for a while.

Soon after, Lucetta decided that she wanted to have a baby, but Dave was adamant that they couldn't afford it (yet he'd actually been promoted at work). He also insisted that she was too sick. He restricted her from going out more and more, especially if she wanted to see some of her former colleagues she'd become friendly with. She wasn't allowed to go out to shop - he had the groceries delivered. After all, he countered, did he not work in a grocery store? There were no luxuries in the goods delivered. He criticized her cooking so much that, eventually, she broke down, screamed, and sobbed, and thereafter he said that he would do it, as "she wasn't coping." Soon after that, she went to the doctor, at his behest. Dave thought Lucetta would need anti-depressants. She had them prescribed for her but was also recommended to see a counselor. This was when she was asked: "Do you think your husband WANTS you to be sick?" and, "Do you know what sickness the doctor diagnosed you of having?" With help, Lucetta began to see that she was being controlled and... gaslighted. It had all started not with Dave, but with her own family!

It may be that your own story is different; but whatever it is, think about it using these questions:

EXERCISES: Look at the Other Person Who Is Gaslighting You

Now you can look at the exercises you wrote at the beginning of this workbook. Under the heading, "The Other Person," look at the topics dealing with what kind of things the person who is causing you pain and difficulty now is doing and saying. What did you write? Now ask yourself: is he or she doing things that are the same as, or similar to, when you were a child? Write your answer here.

_____

_____

_____

_____

_____

What kind of things did other people say to you when you were growing up that hurt you or confused you? Is the person you're having problems with saying something similar? Does your family agree with it - have they been saying these things for years? List what people used to say to you and what you've heard recently.

_____

_____

_____

_____

_____

Look at Yourself

The next thing is to look at what you wrote under the topics of "You," the second circle. Look especially at "How Do You Feel?" Is there any time or incident you can remember from your childhood where you felt the same way or similarly? Can you see that there's been a pattern of feeling that way ever since then? Are there any feelings or physical reactions to unpleasant situations in your present relationships that you've had since you were a child, e.g., stuttering, wanting to shut yourself in a room alone, shaking, nightmares, headaches?

_____

_____

_____

_____

Was there anything you had to give up when you were young that you really wanted to do but which your parent/s or caregiver told you was selfish to want? Yes, we all have to be told this sometimes... what I ask you to think of, though, is something that, looking back on it, was really unfair. Is there anything you can see now that you regret not having had, or done, that you were denied?

_____

_____

_____

_____

Have you had to give up or change your plans to please someone in a relationship recently for their convenience? Can you see similarities, and is there a pattern of your doing this to make other people happy that part of you doesn't like because it fills you with regrets? Do you feel that it is your duty, but that other person doesn't seem to appreciate your sacrifice?

_____

_____

_____

_____

Did anyone try to tell you to be suspicious of other family members or tell you that this person didn't like you when it had seemed that they did actually like you? Did you accept what you were told? And, looking back, do you wonder if it was actually true? Was it maybe because your parent or significant other was jealous of that other person?

_____

_____

_____

_____

CHAPTER 3:

GASLIGHTING IN THE WORKPLACE

Gaslighting is everywhere - because the people who do it are all over! A lot of attention has been given to this topic, when it occurs in intimate relationships, by psychologists. This is rightly so, but among the public, there seems to be less awareness of gaslighting in other areas, such as at work. For this reason, I will use this chapter to describe how it happens in the place of work.

Many, if not most people, spend much of each day away from home at work. Even if you're working from your house, especially during this pandemic, you're still likely to be part of some network of other employees and supervisors. Wherever there is personal interaction, there's the possibility of a manipulative, narcissistic type of personality trying to gain advantage over other people. That's not being paranoid: it's just a fact of life.

In any group situation, there can be opportunities to get useful information from someone else without other people realizing it, or make it that some people do more of the work than others, but all be paid or recognized equally. Other workers can be made to look incompetent by being excluded from knowledge of given facts, misinformed, or having false information about them spread around.

Someone who gaslights people at work likes to play games with them, games that only he or she enjoys. There are many issues out there in the workplace, and all of them can be taken advantage of. With much talk these days of employment equality, of more people from ethnic minorities - or majorities - and more women being promoted to positions of leadership, you might be a woman in a previously male-dominated area or someone from an ethnic minority or immigrant background. You just want to do your job. You may find that your fellow managers or workers see you as being a threat. Given the sometimes heavy-handed pronouncements from governments and corporations, e.g., by the year X, such a percent of managers/workers have to be women, of such a background or race, of such an age group, etc., this isn't surprising, unfortunately. This may cause you problems in your daily working life, though in itself, that is not necessarily gaslighting. BUT... A narcissistic personality, basically insecure because of his or her self-obsession and sense of entitlement, will seize this opportunity. A male, white gaslighter, for example, can use his colleagues as 'flying monkeys' to question your judgments, highlight your lack of experience if you're new... Your objection to a certain policy, based on your reasoning, can be dismissed by him as being "too emotional," using stereotypes of how women are thought to be.

The games people play can be distressingly complicated. Given the situations I've just mentioned, there are also opportunities for women and people from minority backgrounds to gaslight others from their own backgrounds! Remember: manipulative personalities of any origin are basically selfish - they don't really have any fellow-feeling for others whose gender, language, nationality, or religion they share. To give an example: before, there was one black member of the engineering project. You've just arrived, so now there are two. Your one black colleague seems very friendly and supportive, but every time there is a meeting or you talk with him, nothing seems to go well afterward. He says he supports a new initiative and encourages you to do so, but at the meeting, most of those present are not in favor, and... neither is he! Then, you find reasonable grounds to support a contribution another member of your team makes, though a few of the others obviously dislike the idea because it involves new technology that they have little experience of. Your fellow black colleague launches the most emotional criticism you can imagine, trying to make you look the fool... Finally, you overhear him, through the walls of an office cubicle, talking to someone and saying that you're very opinionated! What do you think he is trying to do to you? He's gaslighting you. He likes being the sole representative of, let us say, thirty percent of your state's population. He likes to talk to organizations of black engineers (so do you, of course, but he's HIM, if you see what I mean...) with opinions and reflections; and he also likes "toeing the line" and going along with the majority - because it's less stressful for him than working with logic and integrity. You are a threat to all this!

So, what can be said about this? Gaslighting is a result of fundamental human evils you can call narcissism, radical selfishness, or covert ill-will. Such people play an awful lot of games and are found in all areas of work and across all nations. What you have to realize is that though their games are confusing - I mean, the games are MEANT to confuse you - their basic attitudes and techniques can be identified more easily. The exact reasons for their gaslighting can vary, too, but their essential self-obsession, insecurity, and belief in their own superiority are very similar deep down. Once the blindfold is off you, and you can see WHO your gaslighter is, and be sure that you are being gaslighted (or that someone else is), you've won half the battle. No longer will you be stumbling around in the dark. Yes, the other half of the battle is to decide what to do about it and dare to do it, or force yourself to remain calm if you are tempted to lash out in retaliation without thinking. Yet seeing ill-will for what it is, is a glimpse of an uncomfortable truth that is nevertheless very healthy to know.

Think of this: a "Narc," as we can call a narcissist, generally wastes time, from the company's point of view, on his or her strategies and mind-games, such as gaslighting you. So a "Narc" is not as productive as you unless that "Narc" is very skilled, and if so highly skilled, why is that person not in a more senior position? This is one of the reasons he or she probably likes being in authority, actually: not just for the power, but for the degree of isolation from others, the possibility of doing different, more intangible work that you and your colleagues (and other managers) might not be able to see so clearly when he or she is not doing... This is also one of the reasons YOU are a threat to THEM because you don't waste company time like that; and strangely, a reason for them to want you to do their share of the job if they can get you to.

HOW YOU CAN PROTECT YOURSELF

So, what exactly are the tricks being played at your expense, and what can you do? One of the first things is to WRITE DOWN ANY USEFUL INFORMATION, make RECORDS and keep e-mails, list facts, etc. The idea of gaslighting you is to make you doubt your own mind, and because "the weakest ink is stronger than the strongest memory," with written facts, you will be able to remind yourself. The point here is not so much to prove something to someone else (though that would be an added benefit from your records keeping) to help you stay in control of your work.

You can check things with other people at work as necessary if they are trustworthy. Do make sure that they aren't one of your gaslighter's little helpers (called "Flying Monkeys" by some therapists, after the helpers of the Wicked Witch in "The Wizard of Oz"). Such "flying monkeys" may be "ne'er-do-wells" who like to see others doing badly, or they may be innocent - but duped - victims. A very good idea is to talk to people you can trust outside your work because they can be more detached and objective.

Probably you have a right to have written confirmation of certain actions or communications at work. Sometimes we don't ask for this out of a false sense of not wanting to bother others. That's a mistake in this case. Just do it calmly and without any drama. Obviously, there are many different situations at work; and different jobs might not involve much writing, but I'm saying this especially to managers and office workers.

One thing you could do is TALK TO THE CO-WORKER OR BOSS WHO YOU THINK IS GASLIGHTING YOU. I put this for those of you who are still not sure of what the situation is. There is nothing wrong with talking things over with someone in a non-confrontational way; give that person the benefit of the doubt. They might have misunderstood you or might actually be someone else's "flying monkey" out of ignorance. Be warned: if he or she is really the gaslighting type, your talking to them is not likely to go well. Narcissistic types are extremely sensitive; they look for ways to trip you up and are determined not to understand you or listen to you. However, this gives you the opportunity to see that person in their true colors!

Gaslighters' tactics work in part because they isolate you from the people in your environment who could otherwise give you objectivity and help your awareness of reality. So one way to manage working with a gaslighter is to TALK TO OTHER PEOPLE. If you have friends who will listen, tell them what you are experiencing and get to know what they think. If you can try to talk to your gaslighter when other people are present, so much the better (I assume you tried to talk to them one-to-one non-confrontationally, if you were unsure of whether you are being gaslighted, and that now you know, or have confirmed it). Try your best to get on with any other people in your workplace. Yes, they might be "flying monkeys," but that might be out of ignorance. You don't want unresolved conflict with co-workers in any situation, but doubly so when there is a manipulative gaslighter there: the gaslighter can and will try to use it to cause chaos, conflict, and confusion for you.

The Human Resources department in larger companies is there to help workers be productive and co-operative, and ensure that there is good communication between management and staff. Some therapists recommend that you go to HR as soon as possible; others warn you against it. These people could help you to look at your style of communication, perhaps give you some help based on their general knowledge of the company, and in some cases, hear you in confidence. If you believe that they'll be willing to help you, then do so in a way that doesn't sound like making an official accusation against your colleague or yet against your boss. Be humble, and show an openness to talk about how to do your job in the best possible way, how you might consider talking to your gaslighter - or if you have, what their reaction was.

Others say that, all too often, the HR department is there to look out for the interests of the company- this is understood as reducing the number of complaints. If you are the first person to try to call out your boss, it may seem easier for them to say nothing to him or her, or if they do and your boss denies it totally or retaliates with negative comments about you, then they might say nothing if your boss tries to have you fired! It may take time, and several different people reporting problems with the gaslighter responsible, to make them take it seriously. You'll have to judge this yourself.

Simply AVOIDING your gaslighter can help you to stay calm and would remove you a little bit from their observing you. This isn't always possible, but if you can do this - perhaps socialize in the other cafeteria, take a break at a different time - it will help you to cope with the stress of the situation. While you don't want to cut this person out of any information needed at work, in the way some gaslighters do to their victims, you should try to avoid talking about unnecessary personal things in their presence. This is because they take and remember things about their victim to use them against that victim!

You must SET STRONG BOUNDARIES regarding what you will and will not tolerate. If your abuser has said verbally that he or she will return the stapler and hasn't, let everyone know it must be returned! If he is supposed to drive the company bus to take the workers to the train station, remind him if it's time and he's not ready. If that person has to do something, don't go and do it yourself to "keep the peace" because then, you're just being used... With other things, though, try to maintain your calm.

Posing a very INDIFFERENT attitude, even when you feel angry, confused, or worried, is another important way to handle a gaslighter in the short term. Because such narcissistic characters "feed" on your anger, confusion, or worry, you'll be denying them the "narcissistic supply" they want to see and sense in you. Some people call this technique the "GRAY ROCK" approach. Although being firm with other people is a necessary skill (as I said in the previous point about boundaries), firmness isn't about being angry, shouting, or appearing to be stressed. The only thing wrong with this approach is that it's actually playing a mind-game with your abuser - useful though it can be. Games take energy to play and therefore stress you somewhat.

At home and in other areas of your life, relax, meet people, and do enough exercise to stay healthy. Talk about other things than your problems... In other words, stay strong and LOOK AFTER YOURSELF! This is always important, but even more so when dealing with a difficult situation at work and need to stay resilient mentally.

COUNSELING AND THERAPY should have their place among your coping skills... To have someone else's input and point of view, someone who has experience of helping people in situations similar to yours, can help you break out of the vicious circle of doubt that gaslighting can cause to spin inside a victim. Believing that you need help is not a delusion, and deciding to find someone to coach you, heal you, analyze your situation with you, and so on, is not a sign of having a weak character! One important truth to ponder is that you must not be ashamed of yourself once you get to the point of seeing how you were misled and confused. Don't wonder too much why you were the one chosen by a sociopathic person to abuse; don't take it personally when you remember the bad things they've said or had others say about you. It was done out of their need for control, their obsession with their power and entitlement.

One thing I'd like to mention here is the possibility of REPORTING OR EXPOSING the person who is gaslighting you, with regard to some definite, serious offense against others and, or, against your employers. I must warn you: don't consider this if it will only give your gaslighter a reason to hate and fear you!! Such people are prone to vengeance, to retaliating even for tiny "offenses." Yet maybe you will have to risk an attempt to expose their wrongdoing if any behavior of your abuser, to call him or her just that, justifies it. You see, I believe very strongly that the person who can lie, twist the truth, hide their ill-will, and turn others against you, is very likely to be doing other things that break not just underlying moral laws of behavior but also civil laws and company policies.

If you have come to the point where you can handle your abuser calmly and have stopped being confused and doubtful, and are aware of his or her transgressions, ask yourself if other people are. Should you all not do something about it? I cannot tell you if this will be justified or not - seek advice from people who have knowledge and integrity. There is the sad fact of gaslighters being successful at abuse in places where there is no will to manage the environment they are working in, thoroughly enough. They're just getting away with it in the knowledge that they are safe; in such a case, it might be best to remain silent. This is NOT about your taking revenge, and you must tell yourself to remain calm and act as if your abuser had never gaslighted you, but you still know what you know about their other wrongdoing.

At some point, you may have to ask yourself that hard question: can I carry on in this situation? If you've been trying "gray rock" strategies, avoidance, keeping boundaries, etcetera, and it isn't working, or you find yourself stressed with the possibility of being fired, accused falsely of serious unprofessional behavior, and so on, IT MAY BE BETTER TO LEAVE. I'm aware that in the United States, until recently, you could do that quite easily in many places. There was plentiful work, but poor job security, a tradition of changing jobs frequently, and little stigma in leaving - but not every country has that kind of economy or society. It's all changing, in any case, in our virus-affected world! However, I might still advise you to look for another job... for the very good reasons I began to tell you in the last paragraph: the sobering truth is that gaslighting and sociopathic manipulation wouldn't be happening in an entrenched, serious way unless the work environment was a toxic one. One reason for gaslighters doing what they do is because they CAN: they are people who can sense a place with weak or absent leadership, a place where they will be relatively well-hidden from scrutiny. I could wish some managers had their skills! It is true that some crooks come, do their damage, and either go or are exposed and made to leave. Some of the cleverest and worst gaslighters, however, can go on taking advantage of others for a long time, bending laws and ignoring protocols just enough so as not to get into trouble. Discerning what the situation is like early on is a skill that will be invaluable to you. It could give you time to prepare and look for another position or job; it could save you from getting into an emotionally disturbed state later down the road or flying into a rage and making a scene in public - which won't do your reputation any good!

All right; now you have a key to the gate of the "Cloud-Cuckoo Land" at work, to give it the name I used in the Introduction. You can slip out quietly and clear your head or choose to walk out and not return. Let me ask you some questions to focus your mind...

EXERCISES - GASLIGHTING AND YOU IN THE WORKPLACE

What Kind of Things Are Being Done to You at Work?

Looking at your answers about YOU and THE OTHER PERSON, and anything else that comes to mind, write what is happening to you in the workplace, what is being said and done, what comes from other people, and what you are saying and doing.

_____

_____

_____

_____

_____

Why Is Your Abuser Doing This?

It's definitely, gaslighting, isn't it? I'd like you to acknowledge that and think about why this person is doing it. It may just be for the sense of power! However, there might be a clear or at least likely reason for gaslighting you. For example, he or she wants a promotion, and you are a threat because you are being considered as well! Write about what you think, and don't worry if you aren't sure. This is just to help you to focus and understand your situation.

_____

_____

_____

_____

"Fort Knox" You: Defend Yourself!

Now I'd like you to look at the capitalized phrases and sentences in this chapter on how to defend yourself

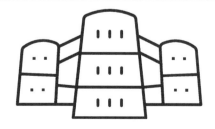

WRITE INFORMATION AND MAKE RECORDS

What can you do, and what are you doing, to keep relevant information that'll help you remain accurate and focused and protect you against confusion or false accusations? Make some suggestions for yourself.

_____

_____

_____

_____

_____

TALK TO THE CO-WORKER OR BOSS WHO (YOU THINK) IS GASLIGHTING YOU

Have you talked to this person? Is there some specific matter you can go to them about? You don't want to be vague or make accusations, but you can go with the idea of asking for clarity or information about what they want, for example. So, what can you say?

_____

_____

_____

_____

_____

When you've done it, come back and look to see if your giving them the benefit of the doubt helped you at least to see this person more clearly.

TALK TO OTHER PEOPLE

Who can you trust and talk to at work about the problems you're having? Who can you talk to outside the work environment? What kind of things would you ask or share? Look at the notes you wrote for yourself in the introductory chapter. What would you like to show someone?

_____

_____

_____

_____

_____

AVOID THEM LIKE THE PLAGUE!

Can you avoid your gaslighter at all? What can you do and where could you go?

_____

_____

_____

_____

SET STRONG BOUNDARIES

You may have seen that your childhood taught you, wrongly, to let other people disregard your personal boundaries. What healthy, reasonable boundaries can you set regarding your work to protect your self-respect and keep relationships with your colleagues balanced? Be specific, technical, if necessary. Just keep them simple enough to enforce.

_____

_____

_____

_____

LOOK INDIFFERENT AND CALM - BE A 'GRAY ROCK'

What sort of things could you say and do to make yourself a 'gray rock'? Are there any words or situations you'll need to avoid if you want this to work? What kind of things have you done successfully so far to stay calm; and, yes, where did you go wrong?

_____

_____

_____

_____

_____

LOOK AFTER YOURSELF!

 Wow, where do I start? There are so many things you can do to look after yourself. Socialize with a... little... alcohol or none, and PEOPLE! Talk about happy things. Visit places, go to a restaurant or make a good meal at home; go on a diet (not a crash-diet, please!) and exercise by walking in the park, the gym, or wherever you like. Listen to music; clean or arrange your flat, or house and garden. Read inspirational books, worship, practice spirituality. Yes, read psychology and self-help books (I would say that, wouldn't I?), but don't wallow in the negative! Come out of the criminal minds section, and read about the art of being thankful for what you have. It's all about eating, praying, and loving, in a way.

So... what could you do? "Brainstorm" some ideas.

_____

_____

_____

_____

_____

_____

_____

_____

_____

COUNSELING AND THERAPY

I remind you that prolonged gaslighting and narcissistic emotional abuse is a serious crime, and you need healing. For that, you really require help. Who can you go to? It would be good if it were a professional; look for his or her experience in matters of narcissism and emotional abuse. If you have few or no paid options, consider an older relative who knows you and loves you. Do you have a minister of religion you can turn to? Are you still in contact with a teacher from your schooldays who you used to respect? Do you have a friend close enough, or with a suitable background, to talk to? Write about who can help. Be specific and name them.

REPORT AND EXPOSE THE WRONGDOING

I cautioned you about this. Yet if there's something serious, illegal, going on with this person - first of all, then you surely ARE being gaslighted by them, as it would be in their character to do so - can you do something about it? Write what, if anything, you think. You could be unsure: it doesn't matter. Answer this question: can I report him/her and know that I'm not doing it out of revenge but rather self-preservation?

IT MAY BE BETTER TO LEAVE THE JOB

What do you think? I've given you ways to help you stay on, but ask yourself what is best — to leave or stay? Sometimes people soldier on, telling themselves that life is hard or that nowhere's perfect (both true), and get themselves into a state of blindness, like looking through the wrong end of a telescope! At other times we are tempted to leave without a fight and are actually just running away. It hurts our pride, either way. The calmest, humblest thing is to look at the situation and come up with some good reasons to leave or to stay. So, I'd like you to put down REASONS TO STAY and then REASONS TO LEAVE. You don't have to make the final decision right now. Just think it through.

✎ Reasons to Stay

_____

_____

_____

_____

✎ Reasons to Leave

_____

_____

_____

_____

CHAPTER 4:

GASLIGHTING IN RELATIONSHIPS – HOW IT KEEPS YOU TRAPPED IN A TOXIC CYCLE

In this chapter, I want to talk about gaslighting and the cycle of abuse in a traumatic relationship. As different as people's situations can be in the details, abusive relationships show an amazingly common pattern of "carrot-and-stick" behavior from the abuser towards the victim. If you are exhausted, upset, and full of self-doubt about YOUR relationship, read on to see how any of the points I describe fits with your experience. Keep the brainstorming notes you made with you as a reference.

To form an abusive relationship needs a victim who is an empathetic personality but carries his or her own inner trauma and woundedness. This was what I explained in the chapter about Gaslighting and Childhood. When you've been brought up to be always on the alert, waiting for someone to start making demands of you, and deep inside you feel lonely and long to be loved and needed, you are likely to attract someone narcissistic. That will be someone who wants love and attention because he or she thinks it is their right and has an inner need to feel superior.

How does the cycle start? Always with a short, intense period called the "Honeymoon Stage." It has this term because so many toxic relationships started with a real-life, "too-good-to-be-true" honeymoon. The abuser is on his or her best behavior; promises are made (usually rather quickly), and love and attention is lavished on the victim. The victim usually doesn't see that the other half is not exactly self-sacrificing: after all, taking a young woman on a "sun-sightseeing-and-sex" honeymoon isn't exactly suffering, is it? Little does the intended victim realize that this is a psychological game to teach her that this is what her beau is like only when he wants to be good or wants something from her.

The honeymoon phase fades, and the relationship enters a time of withdrawal and lack of communication. In fact, in this phase, the abuser starts showing his true nature. Such abusers are narcissists, i.e., obsessed with themselves, and as such, they don't really communicate their inner life and thoughts. To them, doing so is equivalent to showing vulnerability. This withdrawal is used deliberately to make the victim uncomfortable and to start doubting herself. In our example, having a traumatized personality, deficient in self-esteem or self-respect, she begins to think it's because she's failed in some way.

When, after the honeymoon, she asks her new husband what is wrong, the volley of criticism she gets hurts and shocks her. He tells her she looks at other men, her clothes are provocative and indiscreet, her brother's an idiot, her father an ignorant, prejudiced hillbilly... She bursts into tears and tells him she'd never look at another man and think what she thinks of him, that she loves him and doesn't understand why he thinks she doesn't... She says that she's hurt when she hears him criticize her family, but there's an apology in her words when she says she knows they're "not very educated." After this, she tries nervously to be loving, but there is fear in her attitude.

Gaslighting comes into the next part of the "Abusing Stage." If our imagined young wife reminds or questions her husband about his insults regarding her style of dress after their return from such honeymooning happiness, he will deny them: "I never said that. I never called you a whore, did I? I just said I thought that red lipstick was a bit bright..." She's convinced that he said she was dressing "provocatively." He certainly didn't call her a "whore", but he's managed to use the word in her presence, which is his plan. Then later, when he makes a sneering comment that "even your brother could understand that," she asks him not to say bad things about her brother. However, she admits that "I know he dropped out of college, but he's good at his job. Plumbing isn't for idiots, you know; you may think he's a hillbilly, but that's not justified." Then her husband will repeat the famous words, "I never said your brother was a hillbilly. You know what? You're too sensitive about your family." The words, I NEVER SAID!! His wife keeps trying to remember if he did call her brother a 'hillbilly.' She thinks he did, but it's becoming hard to remember what he is supposed to have said...

She tries to be as kind and loving as she can over the next few days, and he rewards her with a new period of affection. One evening, he waits until she's defrosted the meat, cleaned and sliced all the carrots, peeled and chopped the onions, and is just starting to fry them, then he appears in a tuxedo and says: "Come on, darling, let's go out for dinner tonight." His smile is dazzling. She rushes to get ready, and he comes into the bedroom as she's putting the finishing touches to her hair. "That's nice enough, Sally, but... don't you think you could wear something a little more... sexy?"

So, what's going on? I have said that a narcissist uses other people to get things out of them. Whether that is for money, for sex, for influence, or for emotional validation and sympathy, the victim is being used. To be used, someone has to be controlled; and gaslighting is one of the strategies of control employed to gain influence over a victim. The "love-bombing" of the first phase is another part of his or her strategy, and its effect is to give the victim a false sense of hope or normalcy.

Victims keep on desiring to return to the happy moments they think they have had, believing that these were really happy times. This makes them tolerate the intolerable, together with the sense of dependence and weakness the abusive phases create in them when they feel incapable of escaping the soured relationship.

Victims keep on desiring to return to the happy moments they think they have had, believing that these were really happy times. This makes them tolerate the intolerable, together with the sense of dependence and weakness the abusive phases create in them when they feel incapable of escaping the soured relationship.

 Actual abuse begins with insults and negative comments. In the example I've given, where the young wife is accused of trying to flirt with other men, dressing to tempt them, and being insulted that her family is made up of ignorant people—these are lies, and they are designed to make the victim feel shame and guilt, to look within instead of looking without, out to the abuser. They can be quite strange and exaggerated; the idea is that the abuser will repeat them so often that they become familiar. We have a much greater chance of believing something if it has been said to us so many times.

One of the specific reasons for an abuser to want control is because he or she wants to hide something from their victim. The young husband is likely to have plans to be unfaithful to his wife; to get her attention away from his moves and noticing how he looks at other women, he accuses hers. When she reminds him about what he said to her, that is questioning; such people do not like being questioned, and they reply with an attack. Once she is defensive, she's thinking about herself, not about him, if you see what I mean. His denial of his own words is gaslighting; it's confusing her about his insults or hiding from her whatever he wants to keep hidden. If he has an affair in the future, he will use gaslighting techniques to try to convince her that she is mistaken to think so.

The "love-bombing" of an abuser is also a sort of gaslighting in itself. It is so opposite to abusive behavior (and this can include physical abuse) that it is confusing and used for that end. "I never hit you," a violent type may say. "You're imagining it! After all, didn't I pay for you to have new kitchen surfaces and cupboards?" The fact that he DID hit his wife and paid for the kitchen to be upgraded are two separate unrelated facts. The fact of one doesn't deny the fact of the other! The victim is made to question reality and think that the situation may not be quite as bad as it had seemed.

If you are a person who wants love desperately, who's had a childhood lacking in attention or love, it's all too easy to become trapped by this cycle of abuse and to cling to the seemingly good moments, even as they grow fewer.

At this point, it is time to look over your brainstorming exercises again. I want you to examine the topics of "The Other Person": to look at what he or she has said and done. Can you divide it into three sections? Love Bombing, Abuse and Gaslighting.

Love Bombing

What can you see that is a typical "love-bombing" action? Somewhat too good to last? Maybe kindness with a demand made of you at the same time? Or maybe loving, but somehow timed to be awkward or confusing, e.g., offering to take you out to dinner just when you'd already started making it? If you can recall any other words or actions of your abuser, add them here.

Abuse

What abuse have you suffered? Whether mental, physical, or emotional, abuse is a crime, and it is unacceptable. Just write the things you've endured in the cycle of cruelty and insult.

_____

_____

_____

_____

_____

Gaslighting

Now that you have more of an idea of what gaslighting looks like, what examples can you see or do you remember now? Can you think of what the intent was - to hide something or possibly, get your attention away from something?

_____

_____

_____

_____

_____

The hard fact of the cycle of abuse is that although it sways between better and worse behavior, its balance always goes down. Abusers who get what they want do NOT become less abusive; on the contrary, they become more so. Dear victim, don't fool yourself! Male victims mustn't imagine that the sweet, apparently-loving female they fell for is the real person... when she also criticizes him savagely, demands more and more money for herself, lies about him to his family, and tries to turn their child against him.

To return to my earlier example, our imaginary couple will end up as a pair of disturbed people: the husband here becoming dependent on the abuse of his wife to keep up his sense of being lovable and powerful; his wife dependent on him for his ever-diminishing displays of love. Once a victim becomes dependent on their abuser, it means that they start to accept what they are told. Perhaps she'll try desperately to wear plain clothes and not seem chatty or flirtatious in public. She may end up being made to stay in their flat for longer and longer, and his abuse may become physical. Will she end up with him slapping her in the face and calling her a 'whore' because he saw her talking to a male shop assistant while he waited outside? And will he say the next day, "I never hit you! You're going crazy! It's that young drunkard from the shop you're having an affair with! Do you really think you can hide what you're doing from me?" All this time, I ask you, will he have been faithful?

Gaslighters are people who use information against others. Unfortunately, if you are an insecure and trusting person, quite possibly, at the beginning of the relationship, you confided in your future abuser, telling him or her some unhappy personal or family secrets, perhaps. Or you might have talked about what negative things you think about yourself, and you find yourself being made, by way of insults, to feel those very things!

What about someone who admitted during dating that he'd tried to commit suicide because of depression when he was sixteen? Once living with his girlfriend, she begins to question everything he does, mocks him for not standing up to his father and elder brother, and denies that things happened as he remembered them; in short, trying to get him depressed. Perhaps she will present herself to his family and her friends as being an angel who keeps having to rescue him - tries to help him - while in private she sneers at him and calls him a "looney"!

Unfortunately, it's what he keeps saying to himself in his head (and from where he will need help to get out of this habit), and now he keeps hearing it from his girlfriend as well. The confidence has been understood and taken advantage of to make him controllable.

At times, you may feel so fed-up and hurt that you want to leave the relationship desperately, but the cycle of abuse I have explained might have cost you a mountain of shame and lack of confidence. When that is coupled with the confusing tactics of gaslighting, you will feel that you are just too useless and confused to make a change.

You may be experiencing what is called "co-dependency" and "trauma-bonding," which I will explain in the next chapter. You may feel yourself saying, "Better the devil you know than the devil you don't." Don't lose heart: just realize that you do need to strengthen yourself to resist gaslighting. It's serious, and it won't get better if you leave it!

ANOTHER EXERCISE

Looking at the last two chapters: firstly, can you think of any deeply personal information about yourself or your family that you shared with the person who is abusing you? How is it being brought up, referred to, or used against you?

_____

_____

_____

_____

_____

Secondly: have you ever contemplated leaving your relationship, and have you ever said to your spouse or partner that you wanted to leave? What did you think, and what did you say?

_____

_____

_____

_____

_____

CHAPTER 5:

YOU MAY BE CO-DEPENDENT

The first thing I want to do in this chapter is to explain what psychologists mean when they use the word "co-dependent" and how it may apply to you in a relationship or interaction where you've been subjected to gaslighting.

Are you - or is someone you have in mind while reading this book - happy to help other people? Do you feel rewarded when you've been able to make a difference in someone's life? That means... you're NORMAL! Part of having relationships of any kind, part of human social life, consists in helping others.

Yet, are you - or are they - living for no other reason than to be helpful? Is trying to save someone from himself or herself the only thing you can say you're good at? Do you feel worn-out and used by someone, or by other people, but soldier on because you believe that if you keep on trying, you can make them love you or make them better people? If so, then you are "co-dependent" on others.

Earlier on, I took you on a tour of your childhood because this time of your life can teach you certain behavior patterns towards other people that will affect your relationships in adulthood. Growing up in a family with other people who have serious problems means growing up with their problems dominating absolutely everything. Where adults have screaming rows and drunken binges (to name two of the more serious ones, for example) they put all of a child's attention on his or her trying to survive, to cope with it. You learn to put yourself in the background and ignore your own needs; perhaps you learn quickly how to clean up the mess and cover up the shame of your household, by not answering the neighbors' questions, for example.

It's a case of growing up too soon; you have to see things a child ought not to see, maybe make decisions for an adult. You would also get a hidden message that family members with big problems are more important than people who can keep on managing quietly; and that your purpose in being there is to look after, protect and help other people who are hardly appreciative, in many cases. It's stressful and fearful, but you call it your reason for existence: you think happy people wouldn't want you! What a tragic mistake to make, and how subtly twisted it is from real altruism! This is co-dependency. Well, if that happened to you - and it might have been in a quieter way - it's understandable. Perhaps one of your parents suffered from depression and was uncommunicative or confused: you treated them with care, second-guessed their moods, and forgot about your own feelings.

Children can become "people-pleasers" who long desperately to be good enough, clever enough, and devoted enough to heal their caregiver or caregivers. A grown-up "people-pleaser" is quite likely to think much the same, deep down, unless he or she has enough experience of healthy relationships. That means it is all too possible to gravitate towards relationships with people who have addictions or violent personalities or to gaslighters, even if they don't have some of these traits. Gaslighters (who are narcissistic manipulators) will certainly be drawn to them!

Co-dependents (the word used when speaking of people who are emotionally dependent on people who are, in turn, dependent on drugs or alcohol) are not trying to act out of a desire to control people as if they were objects. Their desires can be good, but they aren't the heroes or heroines they think they should be. They need to know how to be happy in themselves, and how they could also give to someone freely, someone who doesn't have to be helped but just likes them. Healthy relationships are as much about receiving as about giving. Co-dependents might fear secretly that if their loved one or significant other really came right, was healed, and saw the light, then they would no longer be wanted or needed. There's an unhappy, vicious circle built into their ministrations.

If you are reading this to try to help someone else, you may have already heard their sad but stubborn reply: "But I'm only trying to help! If I don't do this, they'll never get better..." You may see now, if you know the circumstances of their youth, why they have developed this attitude, and deduce that they are victims. You can't blame them, but you will need to break the truth of their being manipulated to them. They need to learn that their sense of self-worth is important in order to love other people wisely!

If you see yourself in this explanation of co-dependent behavior, your way out of co-dependency is not, therefore, to call yourself crazy - more of that in the next chapter - but to learn how to meet your genuine needs in the right way, with truly empathetic people, and to be loved for WHO YOU ARE, NOT WHAT YOU DO. You survived a toxic situation by being like a servant to unhappy people; now you need to learn how to help normal people as a friend, then maybe as a lover, or as a family member. Then, if you ever help unhappy people, you will do so with an inner calm and not let them control you. You need to set yourself healthy boundaries; when you do, you'll know when to let go of someone if you can't help and when to stop helping them if they don't need it anymore!

Read and think about the following questions: you can refer to the circle of topics called "YOU" if you need to think about how you feel and have been behaving.

Do you feel bad about yourself and only feel better when you know that you are helping other people? If you can't help in a given situation, does it plunge you into feelings of being useless?

_____

_____

_____

_____

_____

When you think back to your childhood, did you learn to be caring and to help someone because you wanted them to love you, but you weren't sure if they did? Who was it?

_____

_____

_____

_____

_____

Do you feel that the person who's been trying to gaslight and confuse you would start loving you if he or she could understand how much you've done for them? Do you feel angry with them but still want to try loving them harder?

_____

_____

_____

_____

_____

Are you the person who consistently gives more of your time, effort, and thought to your relationships than the other person or people do? In what ways? Do you hate it when you have to say "no"?

_____

_____

_____

_____

_____

_____

Are you willing to tell little lies, to give up what you really believe in, just to be able to keep the peace in a conflict? What things have you hidden? What ideals or hopes have you ever given up for someone?

_____

_____

_____

_____

_____

_____

Do you think that, as difficult as it is to live with or work with someone who is gaslighting, that you are afraid of them leaving you or not wanting you? Or, are you afraid that they'll destroy themselves or fall apart if you aren't there to help them? Have they ever threatened to leave, or if it's another type of situation, threatened to fire you, to stop co-operating with you, and you are afraid because you believe you outlive your usefulness?

_____

_____

_____

_____

_____

Does knowing that another person needs you make you feel important? Is it like a job description of your life, that you feel "unemployed" without?

_____

_____

_____

_____

_____

_____

Do other people tell you or imply that they think it's up to you to take responsibility to help the people in your life with difficulties? Which people tell you this? Is that actually reasonable? What about them: can they not help since they were the first to notice?

_____

_____

_____

_____

_____

_____

Do you find it hard to say what you feel about yourself in a relationship, but much easier to say what the other person feels and does accordingly? Try to write about how you feel in the relationship.

✎
_____

_____

_____

_____

Write down what goals you have for yourself in your relationships without mentioning the other person or people... Then ask: was that hard work?

✎
_____

_____

_____

_____

If you can see a pattern of "needing to be needed," of answering a lot of these questions with "yes," then it shows you that you are co-dependent. If you are, don't beat yourself up! It will just help you to understand why you've been so affected by someone in your life trying to gaslight you. You are starting to identify what inner needs for healing you have, that once met, will make you less vulnerable, more confident, and a much less easy prospect for gaslighting.

CHAPTER 6:
MAKING YOU 'CUCKOO'? CAN GASLIGHTING CAUSE MENTAL ILLNESS?

"Sometimes I think I'm going crazy..." Dear reader, so many people who are victims of gaslighting say this! If your abuser, in whatever situation you are, keeps telling you that you're in "Cloud-Cuckoo Land" - from the expression I used in the introduction to this book - you start feeling as if it's true. So, does that mean you must be "cuckoo," i.e., crazy?

Everything in this chapter was written to calm you and help you. I'm going to answer the question truthfully and say, "Yes, it can cause mental illness." The kind and type of illness depend on the abuser, the situation, and you, but gaslighting is done especially to cause mental distress and confusion.

Yet the good news is that ONCE YOU KNOW YOU'RE BEING GASLIGHTED, YOU HAVE WON HALF THE BATTLE. It's actually very relieving to know this unpleasant truth. The other half of your battle - to get back control over your life - is much harder; but with your abuser identified, you can go about finding ways to focus your mind again, connect back to other people, and understand yourself as well as the narcissist you've been 'conned' by! So, read on...

Gaslighting means that someone is trying to tell you that you can't remember things in the sequence they really occurred in, or perhaps the events just weren't so important and that you've over-reacted, or the facts you remember are supposedly insignificant. Despite that, you know, you probably have been abused, insulted, and poorly treated, and to do so is wrong and can only be an expression of someone else's ill-will towards you. You have to accept that you were treated badly and resolve to find a way out of the mess of confusion your abuser has created around you. Once you see that someone's trying to confuse you - I repeat - that's half the battle won!

Gaslighting starts small and works from there. This is the first thing to understand about mental distress. For example, if you're suddenly told for the very first time that you're a selfish monster who enjoys punishing your loved ones and that you don't love your own children as much as the person who is insulting, criticizing, and confusing you does... you will be upset, but think your accuser is crazy, and you won't accept what he or she says.

Yet, if that person makes you question whether you disciplining your child in one particular situation was done out of selfishness... you may start to wonder. If this is repeated in various ways over time, it may start to make you doubt your motivations. Then this doubt will be exacerbated to disorientate you. Eventually, with their threats and anger and your guilt, you might have given in and accepted that you are selfish and don't love your child... as much as your insulter and manipulator does. You will hear the full accusation of, "You're a selfish monster who enjoys punishing your loved ones, and you don't love the children enough!" only later on.

You give in... the goal of all this is to make you surrender judgment. You are told to accept your abuser's opinions because you are untrustworthy and "crazy." What should you do? DON'T give in: you need to use your judgment because it's your God-given gift of reason, and you have a right to do so! It's your sense of self, and you need it to live healthily. If you surrender your judgment, you open the door to depression, stress, alienating yourself from other people, and all manner of unhealthy states of mind. Even having mental illness or distress is not an excuse to let go: rather, it is an unpleasant situation where what you need is to calm down and find a way out of it, as with any other problem. Don't fear! It's not the end of the world!

Be aware of your own body: do you feel stress and pain when you are in someone else's presence? Do you keep analyzing what they said even long after they've left? Are there patterns that keep repeating, such as your trying to express your unhappiness with their behavior, which ends with your apologizing for yours instead? That would be an example of their shifting the blame back on to you and away from what THEY did or said. It's bad... yet if you can see it, then you are protected by teaching yourself to recognize that it's THEIR avoidance and their problem, not yours.

To have a therapist or counselor, or to have friends, anyone at all who can comment kindly on what you say will help you to be objective and calm. Part of gaslighting is precisely to cut you off from other people, to try to stop someone else from standing up for you, joining you in a complaint about your abuser's bad behavior. If you can benefit from someone else's viewpoint, you are resisting the gaslighting...

A piece of good advice to victims, who tend to feel a lot of shame and self-hate, is that gaslighting is not to be taken personally, nor is it something you blame yourself for. Narcissistic manipulation is born out of a narcissistic person's pathological - sick - need to control others. Whoever the victim is, they tend to be treated in a very similar way!

Protecting yourself against future "gaslighters" in your life or further damage from those who have already done this to you can get a boost when you realize that you shouldn't let people too quickly into the most intimate or personal parts of your life. It takes time to build up trust and mutual acceptance. Manipulative people use the "honeymoon phase" of a new relationship to force you to open up too quickly and too much on your side... without a corresponding openness from theirs. When you can see these tactics and identify who is using them, you can resist them.

There is another way they try to control you. Some people call it the "Goebbels Tactic": it's when your abuser accuses YOU of all the things he or she is doing (named after the Nazi Cabinet minister who would accuse the Allies of all the things the Nazis were doing). Most commonly, your abuser will try to play the victim. If you react with anger or irritation to their confusing strategies, they know they have succeeded in having an effect. At once, they take this defense to be an attack on their person, and accuse you of being the aggressor, and make out that they are victims. You need to say to yourself that it doesn't matter what they say because you know within yourself what the truth is.

It's so human to want to explain yourself, but here, it's of no use and actually weakens you. Your abuser doesn't CARE what the genuine reason for your reactions is: he or she just wants to use them against you! If you want to have an extra portion of rice because you feel you will need the energy, stick with that. Don't let anyone make you feel guilty. Trust yourself a little more!

Yet another life-preserving and energy-saving skill you can learn is to accept that with some people, you can never have an adult, free and open conversation! Manipulators just do not have normal, balanced, two-way, mutually respectful dialogues with people they consider prey. You will have to watch what you say, keep it to a minimum, and not overthink their words. You'll need to say what you have to say and not become too emotionally involved.

When it's necessary to set boundaries, to make a statement, try to do so without fear of the abusive person's reactions. You know why you've decided to set your boundaries, so be strong and draw a line in the sand. Don't let your abuser's reactions set the pace. You are, in effect, allowing the other person to think whatever they like: tell yourself that it doesn't matter. They don't need you to convince them because they don't care what you think (unless they can use it to pull you down)!

Perhaps, dear reader, you've been gaslighted for a long time: it is to be expected that you'll have issues. Maybe you find it very hard to trust other people again; maybe you feel a lot of shame and lack of confidence. You have probably cut yourself off from people who might once have supported you. You'll need to recuperate these areas within yourself and with other people, and it will take time. Give yourself that time, and seek to understand and be healed within your mind as you try to rebuild your sense of self, as opposed to the false caricature of yourself that your abuser wanted you to be. If you hear voices in your head, you need to identify if it's the real you; or just a "superego" disguised as a sort of fake conscience, tricked into being your abuser's servant. Anything you can do to live by your convictions and look after yourself will strengthen your mind and make you mentally healthier. That's the opposite of being crazy!

CHAPTER 7:

HEALTHY RELATIONSHIPS VERSUS NARCISSISTIC RELATIONSHIPS

It is time to examine some of the important differences between a normal, healthy relationship and a manipulative, especially narcissistic, relationship. The emphasis will be on intimate relationships, but one can draw conclusions for other kinds of human interactions.

The reason for this topic is to help you understand the situation you were in when you started being gaslighted and how it regressed from there.

If you compare a healthier relationship to what you've endured, you'll be equipped better to understand and defend yourself in the future, whether your abusive relationship is still ongoing or has ended.

Narcissistic relationships, to call them that, or anything manipulative in tone, start differently. They start off, almost without exception, being just "too good to be true." Imagine the first time you agreed to go out with the tall, dark, handsome fellow if you're a woman, who was a stranger till yesterday. He arrives at your door with a bunch of flowers, a huge bunch of flowers. Definitely giving the impression that this could be the start of something big.

Do you realize that the vast majority of people who fall in love, stay together, get married and remain happy together started their relationship quite casually? You could prove this by asking around. Maybe, if you're a man, you were just talking at a work conference, and you mentioned to her that you like salsa-dancing. She says, "Really? I'm going to dance classes, and we really need another man to practice with. There's not enough of you around to have a partner!" When you arrive there, she introduces you pleasantly but quite casually. She's dressed for dancing - practical shoes - she's pretty but not "dolled up," and afterward, you chat together. You arrive the next week, and it's the same, but you decide that you like her, and the dancing classes too! Your first date will probably happen only a few weeks to come and have you vaguely nervous, wondering if this might go further. When the time comes, she arrives on time, and you have fun during the date. At the end of the date, the bill is brought, and she requests to pay for hers, but you reply, "No, that's all right; it's my pleasure."

I hope that these examples illustrate the differences. Would a manipulative person show any warning signs at this point? Perhaps the big show he or she puts on will be causing strain.

IImagine that pizza "arrabbiata" is on the menu but is not available that evening. 'TDH' (tall, dark, handsome) snarls at the waitress: "Why?! What's the point of printing the menu if something's on it but not available?" You might assume it was because you, his date, were so important to him that he wanted the best for you and was afraid of not getting everything right. Maybe so, but is his outburst making you happy? Surely he'd want to be on his best behavior? Understand this: maybe that is 'TDH' on his best behavior. His best behavior is having a few flashes of irritation: might his worst be giving you a black eye or trying to strangle you?

I don't want to make anyone paranoid. Being gaslighted is bad enough. Yet if you are in the situation of being gaslighted, or abused emotionally or physically in any way, for some time, look back to the beginning of your relationship with this person, and see how early the warning signs you read were exhibited.

A typical characteristic of these manipulative relationships is their "love-bombing," as it's called. You get open, almost theatrical displays of affection, as we have discussed. What if the generally loving, over-the-top emotions of this person seem to reach out to the whole world? You might see them greeting everyone as if long-lost friends, kissing (in the pre-Covid-19 world), answering a call from his mother with words like, "Yes, my darling Mamma!" So, that's all very well and good; but does this general goodwill not tell you that you, the one 'TDH' invited for a date in a very good restaurant, are only getting what he gives to everyone? Once again, does one of the phone calls get a very unpleasant reply? Or does he look to see who it is (the 'phone isn't on silent: does he really have to be 'on call'?) and press "reject" angrily when he sees the name? These are things to think about carefully and calmly if you are embarking on a new relationship.

I used the words "carefully" and "calmly." That sort of feeling, if you get it in someone's presence as you begin to know them, is a very good sign. Narcissists and people who are vulnerable tend to generate a lot of excitement when they come together in the first stages of an intimate relationship. That sounds good, but on closer examination, it's stressful nervous excitement like nervous laughter or a roller-coaster ride. Going back to what I mentioned before, are the words and deeds of your new "flame" - if all this is new, or were they, with the person you've been mistreated by for a long time now - somewhat exaggerated? Did you catch yourself thinking it was a little 'tacky'? A narcissist who isn't hidden or extremely shy may very well be somewhat flowery and boastful. Why are such theatrics successful, then? It's a really important matter to realize: it's because of their excessive self-confidence and feeling of superiority. Other people - normal ones - would shrink back if they tried some of the bravado that these people dare themselves to put on and so don't get away with it.

Rushing a very new link to another person on a deeper level is a characteristic of an unhealthy relationship. Is Hollywood to blame for people thinking a good new relationship has to be terribly exciting and dramatic? Even when a normal relationship becomes exciting, it doesn't seem like everything has to be in a hurry. Narcissistic or generally selfish individuals try to rush things because they are insecure and fear losing what they want. They also feel entitled to it and don't see the need to get the agreement of the other or why they should be made to wait. Yes, for anyone, sex will be great; finding a home together, a lot of fun - but isn't "getting to know you" also fun?

Apologizing for something is healthy when it's called for. It's normal as long as it isn't excessive. Unfortunately, people-pleasers and those who were traumatized in childhood, those who are shy and have a low self-image, all tend to apologize too much. From what you've been reading so far, would you say that you're one of them? I'll ask this again later.

People who abuse others tend not to apologize - unless they are "love-bombing" when suddenly they tend to go overboard. Thinking about the restaurant example: when 'TDH' nearly bit off the head of the waitress on your first date, did he apologize to you as she walked away? Or was it as if it'd never happened? I'm almost willing to bet that 'TDH' didn't say "Sorry"!

As time goes by, and dating blends into the time when people can call each other "my new girlfriend" or say "Jake and I," for examples, does it appear, did it, that your other half is running low on energy, and less enthusiastic; and may be less inclined to hold back anger or impatience? Very importantly, have you ever tried to bring up this concern? If you did, what happened?

If your new boyfriend or girlfriend reacts with instant anger and denies what you say or turns it into a counter-accusation made against you, you will have had one or the other, or both, of two classic gaslighting strategies used on you. Such denial can be blatant and total, or they may seem to agree, then go on to tell you that you haven't remembered or understood correctly. By the end of the conversation or argument, they'll have denied it totally. Neither a flash of anger nor a twisted denial is a sign of respect for you. Their anger is part of the reason you would have complained in the first place; their evasive denial of what happened, an attempt to say that you aren't telling the truth.

Counter-accusation is very common if you challenge an abusive or arrogant person. Maybe most of us resort to it at times, but a narcissist will use it instantly and without relent. It can be something about you that is true or total, utter nonsense. Literally, it can be the very thing you've challenged them about... This is a classic gaslighting technique.

To use some examples: perhaps 'TDH' has an unpleasant habit of making fun of people, especially the lowly or weak. Maybe you were together at a photographic society meeting, and the cleaner came in and moved about in the background. She got hold of some buckets, and it made rather a noise. She has a very noticeable limp from an old injury to her leg. He called out to her, "Hey there, Wobble-Walker! If you need to clean the toilets, just make sure there's nobody in there, first." It causes a ripple of nervous laughter to spread across the room, for 'TDH' is a strong influencer of others in a public setting. You are very angry and disappointed with him. When you challenge him about it the next day, saying, "You made fun of her in front of the whole group!" he just says, "Really? I don't remember that. When? At last week's meeting?"
"No, last night."
"I can't recall that. I mean, the cleaner manages to time her coming into just about every meeting, doesn't she?" This latter is beside the point - it's said precisely to move you off the point!
"You made fun of her. You called her 'Wobble-Walker' and tried to make people laugh at her."
"I wouldn't call anyone that name. Who says I did? When is it supposed to have happened?"
"Last night! How would you feel if you had a damaged leg, and people laughed at you?"
"Hang on! I think I remember now what you're referring to. I heard the noise of buckets falling over, and then everyone else was laughing. I didn't understand what was going on, so I turned to look, and then I realized why."

Note the "sting in the tail" here - he's not only denied calling her a derogatory name, but he's accused everyone else (that includes YOU) of laughing at her - and made out that he is the only one who wasn't laughing at her!

So: what kind of situation would a healthier relationship find you in if you had to challenge your loved one? It can happen; normal people can make fun of others when they shouldn't.

Imagine Mr. Average (Mr. A) in place of 'TDH'... When the cleaner comes in for the fifth meeting in succession and makes a lot of noise, Mr. A. loses his patience and says, "For goodness' sake! Do you really have to come in every time we have a meeting? Can't you wobble off to the waiting rooms in the western wing and clean there while we're in our meeting?" A couple of people burst out laughing at his rather sharp wit, then restrain themselves. The next day you confront him, saying, "You made fun of her in front of the whole group!" "I suppose I did. I'm getting fed up with our being disturbed every week," he says.

"That wasn't very kind of you to say she wobbles when she walks! You were cruel."

"Sorry, I can see why you were upset. Isn't there some way we can stop this from happening? Maybe request the cleaning cupboard be moved to the main kitchen... what do you think?"

Although Mr. Average doesn't seem to be planning to apologize to the cleaner (if he did, maybe I'd call him Mr. Better-Than-Average...), he has done so to you. He certainly hasn't denied what he said, and he's trying to express the irritation he's been feeling as a reason for what he did. When he asks you what you think, he's actually asking for help. 'TDH' would never do that (you could actually say that his initials stand for "Too Damn Haughty" since I don't mean to imply that being tall, dark, and handsome makes you a gaslighter). In contrast to Mr. A., 'TDH' sees no need to explain himself and refuses to take any responsibility at all. He actually calls you a liar. His irritation is really very mild because he relishes the chance it gives him to ridicule someone else and control a group. When people laugh, even though they try to stop it, he knows that he has power over them.

In day-to-day conversation, once you get to know 'TDH,' do you notice that he takes very little interest in what you say but expects you to pay attention to him? Does he come late to a date, with no explanation, or an off-the-cuff word of apology: "Sorry I'm late?" All of these point to a deep, inner selfishness. What about you? Does it make you a little uneasy? After all, you aren't stupid. Yet do you find yourself making excuses for someone like this? Have you, or did you notice that you feel the need to apologize rather often? That could also be the start of something big and bad for you.

A good relationship involves a lot of learning about each other. Saying that sounds almost as if it were a series of after-school classes, but it's more like the photographic society. It's learning for fun, and it is very different to the constant flow of information a narcissistic, would-be abuser gets out of his or her intended victim; whereas there'll be a slight, nervous evasiveness when the narcissist is asked about something personal. You won't worry if you've said too much when you're with a good person: you'll feel very comfortable instead. When you say something's important, you feel as if the other person has heard you, rather than just taking this fact away and storing it for later use.

What about relationships coming to an end? Narcissistic relationships aren't the only ones that end before death: a healthy and normal relationship can die, too. Perhaps two people never really became any closer and realized that they weren't truly compatible. Yet usually, there is a sense of thankfulness for what was good and fun in that relationship. A pathologically selfish person will behave badly, whether he or she started the break-up or you did.

Let us take the case of your leaving a narcissistic spouse or partner. The commonest reaction would be anger, threats, attempts to intimidate or sabotage you; the next common might be tears, accusations, and insults. You've been thought of as a possession, and possessions shouldn't be able to give themselves away! Severely physically abused victims need to find shelter in such a case, for a dangerous narcissist will be worse if angered. Narcissists are people who play games, and your leaving them looks very much like losing a game. They will try a great variety of tricks to stop you, or if not successful, to take some kind of revenge, even if it's just by insulting you and robbing you of whatever peace of mind you have left. There's one strange set of circumstances in which they try a totally different approach: they just give in! Perhaps they've grown tired of you without you realizing it. You can go your own way... They may just try this to see what you'll do. One last thing to take into consideration is that a narcissist who fights to keep you from leaving, on failing, often seems to rush off and find someone new extremely quickly. If that happens, you can only wonder what love was lost, if you could be "replaced" so fast!

In the case of the abusive partner leaving you, things are somewhat reversed, I suppose you could say. More often than not, you will be dumped quickly and unceremoniously because there is someone else already. You may have a sense that it was planned from some time before. As with the case of the victim initiating the break-up, there's the exception: the total opposite behavior, where they fight and curse and cry, accusing you of wanting to desert them - and after some time of this, they leave you, and it can be seen afterward that they planned to do so for some time, as I just said.

After an abusive relationship is over, you may feel some relief and peace. You'd be entitled to. However, being as damaging as they are, you may end up feeling awful as the addictive cycle is broken now. In the chapter on gaslighting in relationships, I've already outlined the cycle of abuse. You will need to heal and grow after all you've gone through and find where you've been vulnerable. You'll have a lot of unpleasant memories that may keep coming back to haunt you, called "flashbacks," which have to be dealt with; otherwise, you may struggle for years. How different all this is from a healthy break-up; with a few tears and warm memories, the wish that your loved one may find someone to be happy with, in the way you two were not able to be, you bounce back to your old self!

If two people have children together or children are brought in from a previous relationship, the children can put an enormous strain on the relationship. If it's healthy, it will grow and deepen, but if not, it may break the relationship up. A narcissist is just not going to be the best of parents, whether they abuse or spoil a child. Any parent will feel the instinct to protect his or her child, and if the other partner is abusive by nature, then conflict will escalate. The only way to stay in such an arrangement, and I understand this is sometimes unavoidable, at least for a time, is to set strong boundaries as to how any child in it is to be treated. These boundaries will have to be fought for - but fought in as undramatic and calm a way as possible. Narcissists so often use children as weapons, "flying monkeys," and as bait. A child in such a 'tug-of-war' will need some strong, loving connection with other people than just a narcissist and a victim-parent in order to have some safe space and real love to grow up with. Grandparents, friends, other family members, for example, would need to be involved in the child's life.

A few more points to think about if you are still in a relationship that hasn't ended are looking at activities that you do together and asking yourself if they really are done together. Does your husband come with you to the final night of the school quiz competition to see your daughter on the winning team? If so, did he come throughout the competition, or did he use the "don't have time" excuse? When he does come with you, does he seem proud of your daughter and give her praise, or does he wander off on seeing a couple of colleagues from work and start talking business with them?

If you go to a family gathering of your family, does he come, but look bored and irritated all the time? These days people have the perfect excuse: their mobile phones. Does he just sit there and scroll through it non-stop until he turns it off and remarks: "I think we'd better go now?" That which is not about a selfish character is of no interest to a selfish character. If you are being gaslighted by this person in addition to this kind of behavior, how much more easily do you know that it's a toxic situation!

If you take part in something your narcissistic partner is doing, you can be sure that he or she will be deeply absorbed in it, and you'll be left out or just have to tag along. Imagine a young man who goes with his partner, Mr. Dash-Off Dandy, to Paris, and his partner says that they'll go to a famous nightclub. Once they arrive, Mr. Dash-Off Dandy introduces Mr. Ain't-Got-a-Penny to someone he knows, rather in a hurry. Then he looks around and exclaims, "I can't believe it! Monsieur So-and-So's here. Just wait here a minute - he doesn't speak English." One hour later, feeling rather stuck with his acquaintance (who doesn't speak English very fluently), Mr. Ain't-Got-a-Penny realizes that he's been deserted. His partner just dashed off and left him...

To continue with this example: what might living with Mr. Dash-Off Dandy be like? In my mind's eye, I see a perfect flat in London with all sorts of high-class furnishings. Mr. Ain't-Got-a-Penny will be made to feel like a guest, at best, and a servant, at worst. Will there be space for his belongings in the flat or just a room to put them in? If he puts his dressing-gown over the back of a chair with D.O.D.'s suit-jacket over it, will D.O.D. flip out and snap, "Don't put your sweaty clothes over my jacket!" or look disgusted?. Will Ain't-Got find himself shouted at for getting a champagne-flute from a shining cabinet? "Don't use that! It's Waterford Crystal!" And will he ever find himself polishing the said Waterford Crystal because D.O.D. is desperate to have everything looking perfect when his honored guest, Monsieur So-and-So, arrives from Paris to stay?

Breaking up is hard to do and even more so from a narcissistic relationship because if you've been gaslighted, you've been confused. Whatever your situation is, I hope that you have learned something about what a healthy relationship is, in contrast to a gaslighted experience and, or, an otherwise-abused one. Looking at both the lists you wrote about yourself and the other person, ask yourself these questions:

Did you have a "honeymoon stage" in your relationship? Describe it in a few words, if you did. In what way can you see you were "love-bombed"?

_____

_____

_____

_____

_____

_____

_____

What were the first signs that made you alert to something being wrong or confusing about the other person's behavior? How did it make you feel?

_____

_____

_____

_____

_____

Did you ever feel that you were being rushed in the first few stages of your relationship? In what way?

_____

_____

_____

_____

_____

_____

Do you ever look back on the first, dramatic, maybe romantic, experiences you had? Do you believe that you'll ever have them again?

_____

_____

_____

_____

_____

_____

We all need to apologize sometimes. However, do you think you apologize too easily? Have you ever tried to talk about a concern you had over your partner's behavior, only to end up apologizing for yours or at least feeling bad about yourself?

_____

_____

_____

_____

_____

_____

_____

Look at your notes on "what they said. " what kind of denial, diversion tactics, and counter-accusation do you see? Give yourself time to look at these three areas, and write as much as you can. Look for the patterns demonstrated in the chapter.

_____

_____

_____

_____

_____

_____

Do you see instances when your abusive partner has no time for important events in your life or concerns but an awful lot for his or her own in similar situations? Describe them.

_____

_____

_____

_____

_____

_____

This one-sided selfishness is not to be confused with shyness. Can you see when they became very interested and engaging because something or someone was important to them but still left you out of it? Describe what happened.

✎

_____

_____

_____

_____

_____

If you are still in the relationship: have you ever threatened to leave? How did he or she react?

✎

_____

_____

_____

_____

_____

When you read about healthy relationships, do you feel motivated to leave? Do you think you're staying in it just because you don't have another option?

_____
_____
_____
_____
_____
_____

If you have left this relationship or at least distanced yourself enough, answer this: how did the break-up go? Describe it as well as you can.

_____
_____
_____
_____
_____
_____

Leaving an abusive relationship is the first step to healing. However, you are going to need to heal within yourself. What kind of situations and feelings are you struggling with? Who do you think could help you center yourself?

CHAPTER 8:

COVERT NARCISSISM AND GASLIGHTING

While some confident, openly arrogant, and overly charming people are narcissists, others aren't. They may indeed push and harass people into doing their will and lie quite openly (with total calm), but this isn't gaslighting, and it isn't hidden. These people are known as "overt" or "grandiose" narcissists.

The opposite end of the scale is the "covert" or hidden narcissist. Now, in all of the discussions in this workbook, I have tried and will try to outline different types of narcissistic personalities who gaslight and types of gaslighting.

This is done so that you can better understand what has happened to you, what the person who's doing it is actually like, and what your personal needs and character are. However, I really don't want people to start worrying exactly what kind or classification their abuser falls into or to wonder if that person should be called a sufferer of "Anti-Social Personality Disorder" or not. If you're being abused, try to see and understand what's been happening to you. If you've been or are being gaslighted, then concentrate on getting back your sense of reality, on protecting and healing yourself.

However, when you have a basic idea of what abusive gaslighters are like and some good, different examples to portray them, you should be able to see this person in one or some of them. Some of the official definitions are quite at odds with each other or easy to tell apart in theory but harder to classify in real life. We're talking about human beings, not chemicals! Yet, there are some common characters in this line-up of self-obsessed felons, and you can recognize the types quite easily. Often, you will see your abuser quickly in one or other. And with regard to gaslighting, if you can identify some techniques you've been abused with, well, then - you know you're being gaslighted!

Narcissists who are more covert than overt are dangerous and, in terms of intimate and one-to-one relationships, more dangerous than the extremely toxic, grandiose kind! I mean, if a terrorist tries to plant a bomb in a shopping center, he or she is hardly going to walk in carrying a large, zeppelin-shaped object labeled, "BOMB." The bomb is to be hidden as much as possible. The verbal "bombs" of a gaslighter are their secret weapons, their poison. Let us look at these characteristics more deeply...

These people are quieter, more visibly insecure, much more passive in their approach. They are just as much obsessed with what they want and absolutely no less coldly indifferent to your will or desires than are loud, bossy narcissists. The fact is that, whether grandiose or covert, a narcissist is a narcissist, a fact I think many fail to understand. However, the overt ones don't hide their contempt for you. "Coverts" realize that it's usually far more effective to pretend to be interested in people if you want to get something out of them. Grandiose, overt types either never apologize, or as I pointed out before, occasionally burst out with tear-jerking shows of remorse ("I'll never cheat on you again, my love!" - sob, sob; "I promise, I promise!") which serve only to give false hope. Covert narcissists can fake apologies quite frequently, even admit and identify calmly - at first - what exactly they did wrong. The trouble is that they feel absolutely nothing at all, have no intention of changing, and then start gaslighting you about it - slowly twisting their admission into a denial. Then they will "forget" they ever did any wrong.

Coverts care deeply about their appearance and the impression they make on others. They are extremely sensitive and insecure and can become depressive, which grandiose types rarely are.

"Grandioses" rage at you if you clash with them or criticize them, but often they move on, having tried to hurt or use you just because you were there. Coverts take criticism personally: they don't forget; they keep lists of perceived wrongs and seethe with rage about them.

Yet in all of this, most of the time, you won't realize you've hurt them when it happens. They don't say it. However, they intend to get you back and will start to do it by underhanded means: either to make you realize later on that you did hurt them and feel shameful and apologetic; or while continuing to hide their hurt from you so that you're "punished" without knowing it!

Of all the different breeds of narcissists, these ones are some of the best at playing the victim (especially with those closest to them). They look like victims; in life's ups and downs, they probably have been since no one escapes hardship. When they are, they will remind you of it and anyone else they'd like to know. They are pathologically sorry for themselves, feeling that their greatness has been, or has to be, hidden from the world. Therefore, they love it when people feel sorry for them, especially "flying monkeys" who they use to make others assume that their victim is, in fact, their abuser.

The most important characteristic of these people is that you can live with or associate with one for ages before knowing that you're being victimized! You may look back on your youth, at your memories of people you used to know and realize what they were, only years after. Here are some important signs of a covert narcissist. These signs include signs of gaslighting.

- Coverts let you make a mistake, then point it out. So, consider these events: you are a guest, and you are invited to bring your washing. The washing is all done for you, but you are told, "That was too much, though. You can't expect us to do so much." You are never told what "too much means," even when you ask. Or: when McSlight lets his wife drive them, he says nothing as they approach a badly-placed stop-sign at a crossing on a quiet road, a little too fast. She drives through without seeing it.

Over ten seconds later, he says coldly, "You do realize you drove straight through a four-way stop, don't you?" He's always like that, and she gets into a nervous state from his persistent, unrelenting, but quiet fault-finding.

- Coverts feel very important. They show off by putting you down, denying the reality or value of your achievements, or those who are part of your life. For example, Snearley Snidesdale invites you to tea. You tell her happily that your daughter has won  a scholarship to study law at "Dunchester" University. Snearley says, "Oh, you must be so relieved she made it into "Dunchester," at least. It's a pity she didn't get into Cambridge, though the competition there is, as you know, intense." Snearley's niece studied Chemistry at Cambridge... While many people might just want to say, "Yuck! You're such a snob!" Snearley picks on you because you are a very humble, self-effacing person who's new to Uppity Edge and want to make a good impression on the people in the village. She had seemed to be friendly, in a quiet way...

- Coverts make you feel that their time and effort are far more important than yours, as you can tell from this conversation: "Hi, at last, I've found you. I wanted you to come to my exhibition. Did you get the SMS texts I sent you?"
"Sorry, I don't read texts. I get far too many of them." The "sorry" is very careless. The idea is that the covert is too important to respond to anything but a telephone call or a visit, and you are made to feel unimportant.

- Coverts try to confuse you. Not that they say so, of course. He or she might deliberately say something incorrectly but commonly misunderstood, such as the print shop being in Rock light Avenue when it's actually on the next road, which is Rock light Street. You say, "Hang on - no - it's in Rock light... Street." You don't realize it, but the covert saw your slight hesitation. A few days later, he'll say, "Rock light Street. It is Rock light Street, isn't it?"

"Yes, it is."

"I thought you told me the print shop's in the Avenue."

"No, I didn't... did I?"

"I think we'll just have to drive that way to sort this out. Anyway, it's opposite where that pizza restaurant used to be, not so?"

"No! That's the Avenue. You're confusing me, honey."

"I think that makes two of us!"

- Coverts want to frustrate you. The whole reason for their twisting communications, like the last one, is to exasperate you. When you are in this sort of state, you'll make more mistakes. In that way, you will have to rely on them, and their calm will look good when compared to your frustration. If they want to play the victim, your anger is their perfect excuse.

- Coverts aren't convinced if you try to explain yourself. Naturally, they want you to try because it suggests that you, not they, are the one who's difficult to be understood. The problem is simply that they don't care about your real reasons because they don't care about you. I could understand someone who isn't sure whether he or she is being gaslighted trying to explain himself or herself to a partner.

However, when it just doesn't work, when the abuser just deflects the conversation onto another topic, shifts the blame onto someone else or onto you, you realize that you will never be able to have a normal conversation with that person. This is a tragic mistake of many good people, and if there is still any other person close to you, a victim of gaslighting, they might end up trying to help you by painting a picture of who you are to your covert abuser. They're likely to find themselves going in circles, and the fact is, you'll probably have been made to feel that you're not very capable in communication if you need people to help you!

- Coverts are insincere and cynical. You may hear their critical opinions of others and be hurt enough to try to defend those they put down. As usual, your defense or version of events will be dismissed. However, should you happen to be with the covert narcissist in the presence of a person they criticized, you may find that they display a degree of sham interest or at least politeness. A warning for you: if they talk about other people like that behind their backs, what about you?

- Coverts are very jealous. They are deeply insecure and crave power, so when they don't have it, they fear those who they think, or know, do have it. You can almost see them turning green when they sneer at the rich and the powerful of this world. They are unhappy when not powerful, and so your happiness disturbs them and stirs their envy.

One of their favorite passive-aggressive tactics is a type of non-verbal communication known as "the silent treatment." This is when they withdraw any loving behavior or communication and radiate disapproval and anger without saying what is wrong. I will say more about this later in the workbook. They do this to make you start questioning whether something is wrong, and once you ask, they use strategies such as denying it vaguely and unconvincingly, as if it were something difficult to say - or by launching an attack of criticism against you, with the main point being to ask you why you didn't pick up on their mood sooner!

- Coverts hate being ignored, even though they may be shy, or try to stay quiet for the sake of camouflage. If you are in a relationship with one, they will work to make themselves the center of your attention. Their gaslighting, confusing and worrying tactics all put your attention squarely onto them and how you are treating them. Even your anger and arguing with them is a form of attention, and they actually like it just as much as your loving, nurturing behavior since they are cynics who don't really believe in love, anyway.

- Covert narcissists are hypersensitive. If you so much as dare to burst out laughing when he says, "the gods' gift of immorality" when he meant "the gods' gift of immortality," he will flare up. You might say that many people are sensitive, but narcissists will react with more anger than hurt because their pride is so excessive, and often decide to avenge.

- Coverts project what they feel onto you. If she's happy, then you are expected to be. If she's had a bad day, you must have had a bad day, too. Of course, I add ironically, that doesn't mean that she'll treat you with any sympathy or empathy: it just means that you'll know exactly how she feels so that no explanation or instruction will be necessary for you to know how to treat her as she wants.

- Coverts, like all narcissists, are people you can never be close to. You can have lived with one for years, but you will always feel that there are things about them that they don't tell you or that you don't see or understand. In reality, they are surprisingly empty, just a psychological space between a tyrannical "superego" driving them to be the greatest of all, and punishing them when they fail to achieve it, and a monstrous "id" goading them to crave more and more money, sex and power.

I just suppose that a covert, "fragile" narcissist wants those last three in a different way to a grandiose, overt type. Money is to be used to feel better than other people, and is saved for the sake of being able to scoff in security, not to be spent recklessly. Sex is to be used as a game to control, hurt, and manipulate a partner or partners; rather than just to be experienced as pleasure, as an Emperor has a harem. Power is used primarily to destroy and pull down others who are or might be a threat, rather than to exalt the "fragile" narcissist openly. That's my view of them.

- Lastly, covert narcissists can turn you into an emotional and physical wreck and stay that way for years. They are less likely to "dump" you than other types, but that isn't any comfort to know.

Below are some questions to help you see if your gaslighter is a covert narcissist type and what tactics you've suffered from that you need to identify and start resisting.

Would you describe your partner/this person as an introvert, or extrovert, or somewhere in between? Does he or she prefer small groups and find large crowds or parties tiring?

_____

_____

_____

_____

Introverts can enjoy being with lots of other people, but it takes energy out of them. They can go on much later and longer on their own, or with a few other people.

How does he or she correct your mistakes? Is it maybe passive, negative criticism; or open insult? What happens if you try to correct or disagree with them?

_____

_____

_____

_____

_____

Does he or she put you down, demean you or others, with superior-sounding comments and/or snobbish, pitying, condescending? Describe them.

✎ _____

_____

_____

_____

_____

_____

Does this person expect you or anyone else to keep time and stay faithful to their arrangements or meetings? Does this person reciprocate this behavior? Does he or she try to sound too busy to pay attention?

✎ _____

_____

_____

_____

_____

_____

Does this person try to gaslight you by confusing you with details, changing plans, questioning your memory, etc.? Do you ever become angry and irritated? How do they respond to your irritation? Are you feeling confused?

_____

_____

_____

_____

_____

Have you ever tried really hard to explain your actions or motivations to them? Did it work out? Do they listen to you and change anything they do as a result?

_____

_____

_____

_____

_____

How often does this person seem negative, cynical, and hopeless about other people? Does it seem that they actually enjoy expressing these opinions?

Would you say he or she is jealous of other people? Of whom? Think carefully: is he or she jealous of you? When you're very happy and say so, what effect does it have on your partner/associate?

It's hard to judge if someone is secretly jealous of you. However, some dismissive comments and bitter asides usually come out at some point, to warn you.

What happens if you don't talk to or pay much attention to this person? Do they complain? Do they demand attention?

_____

_____

_____

_____

_____

_____

Have you ever really hurt this person, angered him or her, without meaning to, by laughing at them? What happens if someone else does? Can they ever laugh at themselves/their mistakes?

_____

_____

_____

_____

_____

_____

Do you think you've ever been able to talk about really deep or personal matters in this person's life, or is it always more about yours? Did you really ever feel that you understood what they think? What about now, after you've read this?

_____

_____

_____

_____

_____

_____

_____

_____

_____

_____

_____

_____

_____

CHAPTER 9:

GASLIGHTING STAGES AND GASLIGHTERS' PUNCHLINES

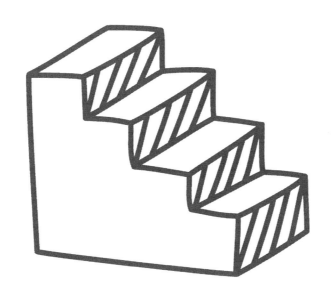

Sometimes it seems as if there is a world best-selling book that has been around for many, many years, called "How to Gaslight Someone to Control Them"! Of course, there isn't, but the most common "punchlines" used by people with narcissistic personalities are so consistently similar worldwide and across decades that it can seem as if they learned it from the same source

It's a case of the human brain working in a certain way, I suppose, and if someone wants to mess with it, he or she will do so by messing with how it works.

I'm going to list the most common ones and explain each of them so that you can recognize how you or someone you know is abused.

That is the easy half of explaining gaslighting; the harder part is to give you an idea of the tremendous variety of ways that a gaslighter can use these tactics and the different disguises they can take. It sounds a little contradictory, but it isn't. Lying is a deliberate attempt to hide or distort the truth, and when I talk about gaslighting, I'm talking about a certain kind of lying.

Before I show you what common punchlines people hear from their abusers, we need to look at the pattern gaslighting, in toxic relationships, follows and its stages. These are not to be confused with the stages which repeat in the cycle of abuse (honeymoon, abusive, reconciliation) between two people - one abuser and one victim. Here we are speaking of what goes on within a victim during each stage of gaslighting.

The first reaction you get, whether someone is trying to bluff you, or you just simply see that something doesn't add up, or even when your partner lashes out and insults you suddenly (as an example), is disbelief. You think it was unintentional and try to think of a reason to back it up. You may question whether or not you're imagining things. You try to excuse the behavior. Obviously, you'll feel a little bit unsettled, but the effect on your mood is still slight. How noteworthy it is to see that you've already started behaving in two ways that are going to become entrenched in you, and which are the very goals of gaslighting, not more or less: questioning your perception of reality and making excuses for the other person!

The second stage or condition is the defense of your beliefs. You would find yourself wondering whether or not something happened or if you've remembered something correctly or not. So you begin trying to work out the truth both within your mind and with your abuser. If you fall for the tactic by trying to reason with him or her, presenting evidence, it actually shows them that it's starting to work! I really mean this: it's pointless trying to reason with an abuser. An abuser doesn't want to be reasonable with you - he or she wants to abuse you. Period!! You trying to be fair and logical tells your abuser that you are trying to stay focused rather than actually being focused, meaning there's a struggle going on in your mind.

Not only that, you're showing them all your thoughts and conclusions, and by laying them out thus, you just give them more opportunities to find a weak link so they can confuse you further. Even the case of a paranoid, alcoholic abuser doesn't justify your wasting time trying to convince them in good faith about your grasp of the truth. They might be in great need of the truth and certainly, want to use the truth for themselves, but they don't want you to have it!

In the second stage, a victim is still fighting the confusion actively. You might be arguing and shouting at your narcissistic spouse or partner, and inside you are striving to maintain your contact with reality. The third stage is when depression sets in. A victim may still want to believe what seems right, but he or she runs out of energy. The emotions of fear, confusion, pain, and doubt become dominant. Basically, he or she has decided to accept the abuser's version of the truth, perhaps as a strategy to cope for the time being. This may bring outer peace for a while (and I tell you, that won't last long...), may avoid another screaming display of rage from the abusive person, or another black eye, but it doesn't bring inner peace. Shame and helpless feelings cause depression, as well as confusion, because these never get better if not treated, but are instead swept under the proverbial rug. There will be confusion because it just isn't possible to believe an abuser completely when they seem to deny that your brain is functioning, yet you can feel that something isn't right.

The third stage can range from mild to as bad as it can be. Victims can become mentally unstable; can end up going to a psychiatrist who knows medicine but, sadly, little of psychological abuse; they can even commit suicide. Dear reader, I'm not trying to sound depressing or make you panic. These are just some extreme cases. The abuser may very well not even want you to sink that low because you wouldn't be useful anymore; many victims keep on resisting, and they don't get to the third stage or don't sink quite so deep in it. Once you know you're being abused by gaslighting, I repeat to cheer you up, that's half the battle won; it's your foothold on reality from which you can start to strengthen yourself again and get yourself out of this horrible state.

Anyway, the fact is that in the third stage, you are being controlled. Such control can never reach 100 percent, but it'll be enough that you serve your slave-driver's nasty, narcissistic purposes. It can seem to be 100 percent control in your surroundings - just don't forget that your mind, your soul, still has a will, a memory, and an ability to reason. Damaged, but not dead! However that may be, the control over you by your abuser can be enough for them to get what they want. Someone to feel bad, so they can feel better; someone to blame when they feel guilty; someone to wash and clean and cook for them without complaining; someone to earn money for them; and so on in a great variety of ways. Control: enough that he or she can, perhaps, get you to lose custody of your children, or get you fired from your job; enough that you lose your temper at the push of a verbal button, in public, so that your abuser can look like a martyr; enough that you sit there in silence and let him or her have an affair that doesn't even need to be hidden from you.

The stages of victimization can switch from one to another or go in cycles that correspond to the interpersonal cycle of abuse. Anyway, what are the "punchlines" that are used to bring all this about? Let me go through the common ones. There are a vast number of other tactics and variations, as I said, but these popular gaslighting phrases are so important and common that I'll leave the others to one side. Abusers can be very predictable. Ask yourself when you heard these infamous words... You can look at the topics you prepared on the subject of "What He/She Said," "What He/She Did," and "What Happened" to help you.

"I *never said that!*"; "I *didn't say that, did* I?"

This first one is a classic! It plays on the fact that we don't always remember what people say (or we ourselves say) verbatim –word-for-word- every time. When gaslighting is involved, however, the abuser strangely has perfect recall when it comes to your faults and those regarding certain situations or persons, and these memories always seem to favor him or her. So even if you are feeling confused about your own memory, you should still be able to realize that this selective, apparent memory-loss of your partner is a sure sign of gaslighting. Of course, this is a way for him or her to deny your own memory, perceptions, and feelings to confuse you. Narcissists don't enjoy being reminded of things they prefer to forget or want you to leave alone, and you are, as I said, more easily controlled if you're confused. The more you hear something denied, the harder it tends to be to keep on believing it: this is an unfortunate fact of the human mind that is used in public life and politics, as well as in more intimate relationships.

"I'*m not angry with you*"; "*There's nothing wrong.*"

When a gaslighter says this, he or she is angry. You may have endured long periods of silence (known as "silent treatment"), or maybe he or she has shouted and accused you several times already. In fact, your abusive partner may be visibly shaking with anger; but denies it. Why? It's another way of making you confused by denying that you see their moods as they really are, another way of telling you that you don't know or understand anything. At some point, they will open up, and you will hear what they want you to hear and see their anger being acknowledged. So if this keeps on happening - think back and remember how often they said they weren't angry when you could see anger, and later they said that they were indeed angry- this a clear sign that you are being subjected to gaslighting.

"*You're over-sensitive*"; "*You're making a mountain out of a mole-hill!*"

Gaslighters say this when they are challenged and when you make an objection. It could be when one partner tries to challenge the other about issues such as infidelity or financial misconduct - in other words, serious issues. Perhaps the abuser is spending more and more money and risks getting you both into debt. Or you may object to constant irritable behavior, and your partner's inability to have a calm, uncritical conversation is pointed out. It's treated as if it were nothing. You are being told, somehow, that other people don't take these things as seriously as you do, that your feelings don't count.

"I was only joking!"

Perhaps someone insults his girlfriend about her big nose, knowing she hates it so much; she gets upset and asks how he can say this if he really loves her. This is a variation of the previous punchline. Everything is passed off as being humorous, even when it is an insult, a lie, or for selfish reasons. Somehow, a victim is made to feel as if he or she is too dim-witted to see that what is said is a joke. There is a good remedy to this tactic: I must point out here that I don't think people with narcissistic or otherwise pathological characters actually have much of a sense of humor. They, not you, are too sensitive. If they laugh AT people, they rarely laugh WITH them. This latter, laughing with people, is what real humor involves. Sneering at other people isn't fun for anyone else, including the victim, obviously - but less obviously, neither would it be for bystanders. So when you realize that your partner really doesn't joke properly (and cannot take a joke at his or her expense), you will be certain that he or she isn't joking. It's gaslighting.

"I think you're having problems"; "You're not coping"; "You need help!"

Perhaps you lost your temper with your abuser. Perhaps you accused your spouse of having an affair, and you're upset, visibly crying. This punchline comes as a condescending insult. Under the disguise of pity for you, your abuser says that you are too disturbed to think correctly or have any grasp of the truth. It's a total invalidation of your reactions. A tactic some gaslighting abusers play is actually to hide, move or misplace some important object of yours. If you calculate that the object couldn't have been where you find it (and how subtle this is, considering that we all lose things...), and you accuse your spouse, for example, of meddling or hiding it, you may be accused of hallucinating, of being not just mistaken, but insane. This is a way of saying that you are the one with problems and not them. This is the next punchline.

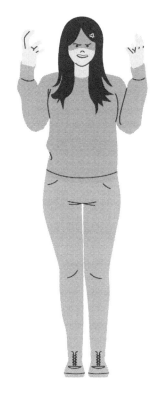

"You're the one causing all the problems!" "You're a hypocrite!"

Gaslighting can be hidden or blatant. When it is blatant, one tactic is to turn all the accusations you make back at you. Perhaps with some even more spectacular offenses added. It's a total denial of the abuser's responsibility. It's a counter-attack that will shift the focus of an argument away from a narcissist and onto his or her victim. The abuser's rejection of your beliefs and your ability to reason is completely ridiculous. The alcoholic wife who had her driver's license taken away for crashing her car while driving under the influence accuses her husband, who hasn't taken a sip of drink for years, of being a secret alcoholic. The philandering husband who's had ten affairs accuses his wife of having an affair. The list goes on and on... Once more, as crazy as it sounds, constant repetition causes other people to accept, at least to remain silent at times, when they are accused of a total falsehood or hear someone else accused. Other people begin to think there must be some truth to the slander if it comes up so often. It's monstrous, unjust, and pathetic, yet, unfortunately, it often works; otherwise, abusers wouldn't be using these punchlines.

"You can't forgive, can you?"; "You have a very long memory!" "I said I was sorry."

Here, a selfish person is asking his or her victim to forget all the things done to them. A certain amount of time, often ridiculously short, is said to be enough to make the misdeeds of an abuser past history. A tiny apology can sometimes be used as a justification for the abuser to act as if nothing has happened. Or, imagine a flatmate who keeps using another one's milk without asking and gets caught with the bottle in her hand. She's shouted at. The next day, she walks into the kitchen and starts talking to her fellow flatmate as if nothing happened. Then she asks if she can borrow some milk. When she's refused and told that it's because she kept on taking without asking, she says casually, "But I said I was sorry." At the other end of the scale, the wife who had an affair two years before is questioned by her husband as to why their mutual friend saw her at a restaurant, having lunch with an unknown man. She denies it: "That's not true. You're being paranoid."

"I don't believe you that easily. After all, you can't deny having had an affair with Mike, can you?"

"You can't forgive, can you? Must you keep on dredging up the past?"

Additionally, this attempts to make a victim feel shame for not forgiving, or better put, forget the wrongdoings of an abuser. Because pardoning is an act of grace or kindness, the abuser twists it into implying that if it isn't done, or revised, then the one who was wronged is mean-spirited or unkind.

"It's all your fault"; "You made me do it!"

A variation of accusing the victim of being the one with all the problems is - when a narcissist is caught or accused - for the narcissist to blame the victim without denying his or her wrongdoing. Supposed reasons could vary from the victim being unable to understand or sympathize with the guilty party, being unstable and thus not capable of bearing to hear the truth, through to the victim being so cruel, so abusive, and so impossible to live with, that the guilty party just "had" to have an affair with a woman ten years younger, to find comfort, for example. This is yet another instance of the abuser trying to play the victim and refusing to apologize. Because this is what psychologists call "cognitive dissonance" - in other words, that reality and what you are told are in complete contradiction with one another - you will feel tension and confusion, especially if the tactic is used together with force or threats.

"If you really loved me, you would..."

This is an attempt to appeal to the victim: to play on the feelings of shame that a traumatized, empathizing person feels so readily. The sense of this expression is, it goes without saying, that if the victim loved his or her abuser, the victim would do what that abuser wanted: to forget the abuse suffered, continue to give love, attention, or money; to ignore his or her unfaithfulness, to remain silent, and so on. It is an accusation of being unloving. If the kind of desperate hoping that trauma-bonding causes victims to feel - hoping that the abuser will relent, will respond to affection, will return to their treatment of them at the beginning of their relationship - is love, which I have to tell you isn't, however well-meant it is - then so often this is a lie! At the bottom of this punchline is a narcissist's feelings of entitlement. A victim has to look at these words in light of what he or she has to bear with from their abuser and ask if the behavior he or she is being begged to allow, or must give love to get, is connected to real love or to permissiveness instead.

There are many variations of these punchlines, but most of them are clearly related to the ones I have given. Look at the words and sentences you've put down under the heading "What He/She Said" as you ask yourself these questions following:

What did you feel the first time you experienced unpleasant behavior or found out about it from your partner? Write words to describe your emotions. Did you especially feel disbelief?

_____

_____

_____

_____

_____

There are three stages of being affected emotionally by gaslighting. Where do you think you are? Why would you say this?

_____

_____

_____

_____

_____

"I never said that!" have you heard this or similar words? Write them down. What was your abuser denying?

_____

_____

_____

_____

_____

"I'm not angry"; "it's nothing." have you heard these or similar words? Write them down. Did you know, or do you know now, what they were really angry about? Was that anger justified? Was the 'silent treatment' the proper way to deal with it?

_____

_____

_____

_____

_____

"You're over-sensitive!" do you feel as if this is true of you? Then, ask yourself if being completely unemotional and unconcerned by your partner's behavior would make any sense. What's your answer?

_____

_____

_____

_____

_____

"I was only joking!" what was the joke supposed to be? Then, put yourself in the place of someone you know. Tell the supposed joke you were hurt by, out aloud, as if to them. Do you think that person would find those words amusing?

_____

_____

_____

_____

_____

"You need help!" has this ever been said to you? Have you gone to see any professional for help? That could actually be really good for you, but an abuser isn't saying it out of wanting to help you. What was he or she trying to avoid talking about when these words were said?

_____

_____

_____

_____

_____

_____

"You're the one causing all the problems!" what were you actually accused of? What were you saying when this accusation was made? If it is really important not to take a narcissist's, a gaslighter's words, personally, then how does not needing to take it personally make you feel?

_____

_____

_____

_____

_____

"I said I was sorry." was that true? If so, what sort of apology was it: casual and off-the-cuff, or tear-jerking? Is either apology very genuine if you look at the way your abusive partner is behaving now?

_____

_____

_____

_____

_____

"It's all your fault; you made me do it!" what was your accusation? Does it make sense to say that you have the power to force someone else to do this?

_____

_____

_____

_____

"If you loved me, then..." have you stayed with this person for longer than you want to? Have you been faithful to them? What serious lies have you told on their behalf? What have you done to be loving to them? Answer this, then look at your answers. Are your actions loving? So, is the accusation of being unloving true? What did they want you to allow/pardon/give? Was it something good and noble for them? Or for selfish reasons?

CHAPTER 10:

MORE SIGNS OF GASLIGHTING, AND WHAT THEY MEAN

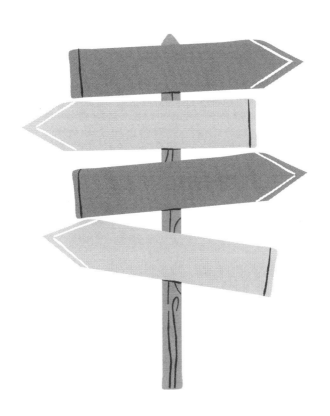

Deep inside, all narcissistic types are highly insecure. We have seen that gaslighting is a strategy to control you, the victim, so that you serve their needs. Now, that is quite easy to see once it is explained to you, but what isn't so easy for a victim or a bystander to see is that they feel a fierce desire to protect themselves because of that insecurity. Your own confidence and your ability to see through their outward "masks" represent serious threats to a narcissist. Let me take you again through some signs of gaslighting, and I will mention some other facets of this behavior you need to be aware of and explain why narcissistic people are employing such tactics.

First of all: all people who gaslight others are people who push, invade, or transgress the personal boundaries of their victims in different ways. They do this in order to control them, and because we are naturally defensive of our personal space, ideas and feelings, our defenses have to be weakened and broken down first. Physical violence is one way, and gaslighting is another (these and other forms of abuse can go hand-in-hand, though in other cases, they don't).

Transgressing boundaries can be done physically without violence or regarding the goods and property of another. It can be done in the victim's mind by crossing logical and rational limits or manipulating and denying their emotions. All of these boundaries can be crossed by the people we interact with in daily life, but to invade them is to do so in a way that lacks all respect and without regard as to how far we want other people to go.

Physical gaslighting, to call it that, is not the same as hitting or punching a victim. It can consist of coming excessively close to a victim and doing so too often. I can only describe "excessively close" relatively because different people have different needs for personal space and keep different distances for different individuals, depending on the level of intimacy. However, we know what to expect most of the time. Touching could be done to re-enforce a sense of over-familiarity, or it could be threatening and intimidating when accompanied by verbal insults. Physical boundaries could be invaded by as simple an act as constantly splashing someone else when standing at the sink, perhaps by deliberately knocking them with a heavy satchel or briefcase when walking past. Is it gaslighting in every case? All of these things can happen by accident or can be done with affection; yet if you've spoken up and said that something irritates, hurts, or bothers - and either it just continues, or worse, it's denied verbally and then just carries on, then you may be feeling the effects of physical gaslighting. Why would someone do this? I've just said it: to irritate you, to hurt you, to bother you. The same applies to damaging, moving, or tampering with physical objects in order to intimidate a victim.

What about mental and emotional invasion of boundaries? These are basically what happens with the classic types of gaslighting. For example, when someone who is emotionally abusive denies what they've said when you remind them about it, you have to understand that your reminding them is a way of saying that you're beginning to see them for what they are. Insecure people with feelings of being superior to others won't like that - so they will try to confuse you, to stop you from working out what they're doing. Denial works in several ways, as I've said. One of the important things it does is when repeated many times, it weakens your confidence in what you have remembered. Gaslighters don't like you judging the reality in your surroundings and are obsessed with trying to make your judgments for you so that you become dependent on them.

When "Paranoid Pete" says to you that you're going crazy, he may very well be feeling a tremendous amount of fear and doubt himself and wondering about his own peace of mind... Narcissists are the world's greatest hypocrites! If he fears that your perceptions of him are correct, it will put him in the wrong and in a weak position. However, as he sees it, if you're confused, and you are the crazy one, he can always be right and be the strong one.

If "Acid Alice" tells you that you are the problem, not her... she may well be projecting her problems onto you. Inside, she is likely to be saying, "I'm scared that I may have problems, but as long as you have problems, you're solving mine!" Seeing that Acid Alice thinks of you as a servant to her needs, your problems are treated as little more than a reason for you to sympathize with and understand her problems. That being so, she reasons in a twisted way, you can get on with the job of serving her. It also makes her feel generous and long-suffering to think that she has to bear with someone like you when she has her own (far more important) worries to think about.

"You're too sensitive!" These words from "Surly Sam" are not a real criticism. While it is true that you can be overly upset when something happens, Surly isn't trying to help you or put things into a real perspective. Being sensitive can imply being aware; being intelligent can help you to protect yourself. There's nothing wrong with that... What does a narcissist think of your bursting into tears? Surly Sam may understand your crying as being a sign that you are aware of his tactics, and he's not happy with that. He may just be irritated - your crying slows you down from performing your duties. More than these reactions, however, he probably feels an inner dislike of your reacting to him as to someone who is callous. It's a criticism, and he's over-sensitive to criticism, actually! However, if your crying indicates that you feel bad, it makes him feel better and more in control, and this is what he enjoys.

A similar sign of gaslighting is when you realize later that someone has been taking notes of your weaknesses, remembering them, and using them later to humiliate you, just to remind you they can. Someone who loved you wouldn't do that! An abuser wants to feel better than you, so he or she will use whatever knowledge they have of your problems and failures to attack your confidence or deny your intelligence. They might make fun of you, for example, all to "prove" to themselves that you are weaker, less competent, less clever than they are.

A sign that you are being gaslighted is when, from your side, you feel a desperate need to explain yourself, after many attempts to do so have failed to alter the behavior of an abusive partner, family member, or colleague. It's only human, but it's a mistake to write a long letter, e-mail, or record a heartfelt audio message explaining everything. Gaslighters just don't listen!

You say: "I'm going to make a great effort: I'm going to lay it all out, without being interrupted, and set the record straight..." You are wasting your time. Abusers don't want to understand you unless it benefits them. An uncomfortable but liberating truth to accept is that you will never have a normal, free, natural conversation with one. It will have to be a careful, managed, low-key communication instead.

What happens when you try to explain? Narcissists use DEFLECTION when you need to talk to, clarify things with, or complain about them. Why do they do this? It's an attempt to avoid dealing with their inner weaknesses and fears, to send your attention somewhere else, and they are very good at it. Consider this case: when Davina Diverger is asked by her partner, Verity, to explain why she keeps hearing that Davina is gossiping about her at work and making fun of her behind her back - Davina replies that Verity shouldn't listen to gossip, that whoever she heard it from is a liar. Verity counters that she has heard this from several people in different parts of the hospital where both of them work. So why is Davina, supposedly her best friend and partner for life, saying these things? Davina replies that it's perfectly normal to have conversations with colleagues. Her partner agrees but asks how this is an answer to her question: is she saying bad things about her or not? If yes, why? Davina vehemently denies it and implies that not only is she not laughing about her partner with them, but she's trying to stand up for her, because they are the ones making fun of her. Vera just feels exhausted and stops the conversation. Once more, Davina comes out looking like a saint, but Vera's not convinced.

Not only does this tactic shift the topic to something else altogether, but usually, it makes a narcissist look better and you worse... In this case, the reaction was devious and quiet, but it is not always the case. Narcissists hate having things pointed out to them, and either they become evasive and deflect them or fly into a rage and try to shut their victims up with fear! In either situation, it is an action (such as I just mentioned in the imaginary case of Davina Diverger) where the abuser thinks himself or herself to be superior to those who share their life.

Another tactic to avoid confrontation with the truth is for a narcissist to use "word-salad." This is what we call uttering words and phrases that have no clear connection to each other, nor to the circumstances! Imagine Davina replying, "Oh, Verity! It's a terrible thing to work with a bunch of liars. You know that Valentine's Day is next month.

These people want to have a Valentine's party, but they don't want you to come. I think people are so ignorant, so old-fashioned. By the way, do you know what the outcome of the Presidential Election is? It's all so frustrating for you just as much as me." Verity would be left scratching her head in frustration. Oddly enough, some psychotic patients, schizophrenics, do this. However, narcissistic types are doing this deliberately. The explanation seems to be that as long as they keep on arguing - or at least answering a query - the conflict is continued because they never want to give in. You, the victim, must be the one to fall silent. The argument need not make sense: if it is confusing, so much the better because confusion is control! Such words as those, in a situation where you are stressed, can also set off a chain of your inner fears, leaving you, not them, feeling insane. Maybe an abuser can make you lose your temper with such nonsense: that's control, while they stay calm...

Do you feel that you'd like to record every conversation you have with your abusive partner? Perhaps you could do it to keep your sanity, but don't bother or even dare to share it. If it would help you clear your own head and remember your actions - well, try it. Be warned, however, that if a narcissist gets to know about your doing this, he or she will act the victim, retaliate, deflect or go off the topic, or just deny all responsibility. It won't change someone of ill will.

Other signs of gaslighting and manipulative tactics are as follows: when your partner's telling you that they know all about you as if they know more than you do! By implication, they call you a liar if you disagree.

If they say something is "normal," but what they say isn't so for you. They're trying to say that you aren't normal because you don't agree with them, rather than appealing to reason. That means they are not using reason!

If they make you doubt yourself, as seen above, or in any way try to do your thinking for you, it means that they don't want you to question what they tell you.

Does this person make you lie - to avoid arguments or fights, protect your children, and keep in contact with significant people in your life? It's a sign of your being gaslighted. Thus, your lying is not malicious, but rather it is motivated by your situation of extreme stress caused by your abuser.

Do your circumstances make you stop wanting to talk to others, including your abusive partner? Doing the latter (as un-dramatically as possible) may actually be a good thing, provided that you don't let yourself lose contact with other people in your life. You may feel ashamed of yourself, but the fact is that you're a victim, and you shouldn't be. Other people you speak to can help you escape the sort of mental prison a gaslighted, abusive relationship can become. Other people can provide other points of view. You don't have to talk about the problems you have with being gaslighted - it's also healthy just to think of other things.

Let me ask you some questions:

Have you become very dependent on the person who is gaslighting you? What kind of things do they do for you or stop you from doing for yourself?

_____

_____

_____

_____

_____

_____

Would you say that your abuser has an insecure personality? What kind of things is he or she sensitive about?

_____

_____

_____

_____

_____

_____

Have you found that your partner has remembered your problems, faults, and other negative experiences? Were these used later to criticize you or justify a negative opinion about you? Write about what happened.

✒

_____

_____

_____

_____

_____

_____

Did you try very hard to explain yourself to your abusive partner? What happened? Do you think you need to try again?

✒

_____

_____

_____

_____

_____

_____

Can you describe any good examples of deflection and of "word-salad" if you've had it from your partner? Write what they said... How did you feel after hearing these words?

_____

_____

_____

_____

_____

_____

You've been reading a lot about gaslighting so far. What do you think is the most important thing you've learned?

_____

_____

_____

_____

_____

_____

CHAPTER 11:

HOW TO STOP GASLIGHTING FROM MAKING YOU CRAZY

After reading the previous chapters of this workbook, you'll have an idea of what gaslighting looks and sounds like. I have explained why people with abusive personalities do it and what they want to happen because of their gaslighting. However, the purpose of all this is not just so that you understand what happened to you, but so that you can stop gaslighting from making you crazy. You need to take back control of your life. Whether to survive living with a partner or family member who gaslights you and maybe others or plan how you can leave such a toxic situation or else to recover after you've cut contact with such a personality - you need help. I'm going to change our focus and ask you to look within yourself.

"The weakest ink is stronger than the strongest memory," so the saying goes. The first piece of advice is to get into the habit of writing things down. What happened? What was said to you? How did you feel about it? How did you reply? All of these things are what you were asked to write down at the beginning of this recovery workbook.

The reason is that you need to stay focused on reality and not let yourself be confused. You have a right to your memory and a duty to use it, so don't feel ashamed to clarify what happened if your abusive partner or family member denies or distorts it.

Consult your notes. These shall be for your benefit, not for your narcissistic abuser's. Remember: if this person doesn't care about you, only about ways to make you useful, then there's no point at all in trying to explain yourself to them!

When you can write down and explain how you've been gaslighted, what proof of it you possess, and how it has affected you and the way you interact with other people, then you'll have a useful and powerful aid to help you stop feeling as if you've gone crazy. The exercises you've been completing all along during your reading of this book and while you've been thinking about your experiences are just that.

One of the commonest ways for victims to feel when they're being gaslighted is: useless, clumsy, or stupid in comparison with their abuser. What can you do about this? You can realize that what you think and feel does matter. If they think differently, then that is their business. Inwardly, you have to learn again (or for the first time) that you don't need to submit everything you do to someone else for validation. Once you can internalize this, it will stop you from collapsing into yet another round of explaining yourself, rationalizing your standpoint, and justifying what you've done. The fact is that these are attitudes of defensiveness, and defensiveness shows weakness when your answers aren't being accepted. It looks like aggression, and it can goad you into turning it into aggression (I'm not saying that to make you feel bad...), which all plays into the hands of an abuser who wants to look cool, calm, and collected - or to play the victim. Meanwhile, you are using energy to defend yourself, and it tires you mentally and physically. That tiredness is one of the states an abuser wants to get you into!

When an abuser denies what you remembered, or what you had to challenge him or her about, then try the following way to respond: if Pushy Patrick says you're suffering from Alzheimer's disease because you maintain that he went out for three hours on Tuesday evening last week, and he asserts that it was under an hour, and it was actually on Wednesday, say: "You and I obviously think differently. I'm quite happy that I can remember last week, and that's really all I want to say." Though I cannot guarantee the results, my point is that you don't want to engage in more and more conversation, so try to close it off in a very calm but firm tone of voice.

The style of a narcissist's abusive conversation is always to retaliate, always to try to have the last word. Your secret weapon is to let him or her have the last word without giving in to their accusations or distortions. If you have to challenge or criticize "Maniac Martha" about what she's done, and you seem to be getting nowhere, in fact, you find yourself being blamed for her actions, you can say: "I think I'll leave it there. We may not agree on who was responsible for sending that e-mail from our department, but the fact is that you know I've spoken to you about it."

Again, I'm going to deal with the question, "Should I leave this abuser? Must I cut off all contact with him or her?" My answer is, "It depends." I need to explain this: if you are really dealing with serious gaslighting by a totally narcissistic person, and if he or she is violent, or has gained enough control of other people to use them to endanger you, then obviously you need to find a way to safety. If the abuse is only emotional - but intense - and you have been seriously weakened and badly affected, it would always make sense to leave when possible. I have to point out that narcissists do not just "get better" or decide one day to turn over a new leaf, nor do they "grow out of it" with age.

Short of a bolt of divine lightning, to cure them, no! However, you may be unable to leave at the moment for many reasons, such as financial dependence, the care of children you have with the abusive partner, a lack of supportive friends, relatives, or an organization to help you, and so on. It's too easy in our throw-away age to say carelessly, "Oh, just pack your bags and sail into the sunset." Although what was done to you is horrible, you may have a reason or reasons to stay.

In any case, if you cannot see a way to leave or reduce contact drastically, the techniques for managing an abuser are much the same. Don't lose hope! What you do have to do is to "leave" your abuser mentally, to distance yourself emotionally. If you can understand what this means figuratively, then you've understood it in principle. This is not some grand decision you make once and for all time, but rather a practical decision you will make again and again. So when you find that you've been drawn into yet another fruitless argument for the sake of arguing by someone who enjoys arguing (and you don't...), then you have to find a moment to cut it off and just stop.

You are actually playing one of the mind games that narcissists play; some of them are quite open about their tactics. They say, for example, "Oh, I never used to argue with my girlfriends. I just let them rant on and on while I sat there, cool as a cucumber." The only difference, though subtle, is that you will not find enjoyment in defying or tormenting your abuser. You will just withdraw calmly and set your mind on other things. You don't want to make it obvious that you are playing a game. Also, you'll be doing so not out of arrogance but from sheer necessity.

By their nature, people who gaslight you are trying to lie to you. Not always directly, sometimes just by hiding things or distorting the truth, but it boils down to lying. If it's true to say that you're mistaken to lie to a narcissist who is trying to gaslight you, it's also true to say that the urge to be totally open with him or her, in a conscious attempt to contrast your attitude with theirs, is also mistaken. It's a sort of fake morality.

Of course, it's not a good idea to lie to an abuser: you have to remember what you said, to waste energy thinking your way out of situations and consequences. In fact, one dangerous tactic of an abuser is that they may ask YOU to lie on THEIR behalf. However, if there is no goodwill in this person towards you or others, and anything you say can be taken and used as evidence against you... then you are morally justified in keeping your thoughts from them. Would you act like this, hiding the truth carefully, to protect your child? You may be doing this already if there are children involved in your life. Realize that you need to protect yourself, too.

Handling a gaslighter is not the same as trying to control him or her. To stop yourself from going crazy - in other words, to stop him or her from controlling you - you really don't need to achieve the opposite. All you have to do is let them think what they want to, while you think what you need to. Have you been deliberately isolated from other people? Have you been accused of plotting against your abuser, of gossiping about him or her when you just wanted the "breath of fresh air" that comes with speaking to someone else?

Have you been accused (often with sickening hypocrisy) of being unfaithful to your partner? You need to focus on the fact that you are doing what you have every right to do - I mean, just talking to people in public or in regular social visiting - without worrying constantly about what your abuser would think. This is not the same as trying to be cheeky to him or her: it's just being free to do what is accepted and perfectly ethical for free people to do. You know what the proper boundaries are: trust yourself to keep to them!

You have to guard the boundaries of your emotions. You know this, deep down. The same applies to your conversations with a person who gaslights you. They evade the reason for any discussion, when it doesn't go their way, or whenever they run out of topics to argue on. What you have to do is to stay focused on the subject. Return to the matter when he or she slips or jumps away from it. Obviously, this is going to be very difficult - I can't tell you otherwise!

Just keep this up until you know that you've said what you wanted to say, at least made your point, and then try to stop the conversation. There's a terrible temptation to try to express all you want to say to a manipulative abuser. That's not possible - they don't want you to say anything they don't want to hear. However, if you keep your own mind focused on the real matter, you will do your own mind a favor, for as it was just said, you can't control other people as a form of retaliation. Really, you don't actually need to!

Children need to be handled carefully, tactfully, and lovingly in any situation where there is conflict between adults, including when one or other of their parents or caregivers is gaslighting you. What can you do to stop them from being hurt and you being hurt with them? I mean, you see a child: a narcissist sees a chess piece in a game where he or she is "white" and you, "black." It might sound a bit insulting when I say this, but I mean it. What you need to do is to have the same calm assurance in the presence of children that you need to have with your abuser and with yourself.

Tell children, if they ask you about it all, that you and your abuser don't agree about some things, but that you love them, and that you're doing your best for them. Say that you believe what you are doing is the right thing. This attitude will do more to calm them than trying to prove yourself to them: children are very sensitive to your fears and insecurities and often see them clearly when they don't understand the adult details of the situation. Tell them not to be afraid and that they can talk to you - that they can... not that they have to.

Gaslighting in an abusive relationship can go on for a very long time, even decades. It can take place at different levels, from in-your-face obviously, all the way to hidden, malignant sabotage of your thought-life and core beliefs. In the end, one of the worst things it does is to hinder you from seeing abuse for what it is, and also makes you hide it. How do you know you're doing this, and how do you stop it? One way to know is to see how often and when you justify your abuser's actions to other people or hide the most upsetting and serious incidents from them.

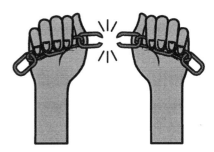

I hope that by now, you can see there is no excuse for abusing someone. If you hide your pain from other people, is it actually because you have adapted over time to accepting and putting up with that person's "version" of the truth? Are you justifying their deeds to keep a sort of peace in your life? Something deep within you wants to keep other people thinking that things aren't really so bad because if they were... you'd have to rock the boat, challenge yourself to take action, risk the wrath of your abuser. When you think like this, you are showing evidence of having been gaslighted.

What you must do is tell other people who will listen with empathy and goodwill about everything you've experienced, leaving nothing out, especially the more unpleasant incidents and memories. Gaslighters have a hidden agenda; find people who don't. It's not as if you are attempting to muster an army of supporters to blame your abuser and exonerate you. All you will be trying to do is find some people you can trust and open up to them. Caring and unbiased people.

You will need objectivity, not just sympathy... When you do find them and share what you've been through, they will react as a bystander would. If you were feeling tempted to excuse what happened but shared it all the same, and they say that what you endured was wrong and abusive- you'd have started to get the help you need to see the truth. If you speak to several people, and they say the same thing... you'll know that they're seeing your abuser's behavior for what it is, and so will you.

Consider seeing a therapist, counselor, or psychologist; above all, one who has experience dealing with emotional abuse. Look at their profile or details on the internet, for example, to see if they are specific about helping with "emotional abuse," "gaslighting," and "narcissistic abuse."

The damage done to some victims can be considerable, and a knowledgeable therapist can make a vast difference. A lot of victims feel shame about seeking therapy, male victims above all. I hope that everything I've said in this workbook helps you to see that being gaslighted is not the fault of any victim, that it's serious, and that it needs certain kinds of help to be overcome. Don't fall into the trap of saying to yourself, "But I can handle it alone," or "I prefer to do it on my own." Yes, there is "work" you have to do inside yourself, but the rest must be done with an eye to the real, outside world of other people and of things.

The practice of meditating or praying, anything that helps you focus, is another way to recover from gaslighting. Not only can such activity connect you to other people if you join them in a church, society, or association, but you can do it privately in your own home as well. You will be able to get the peace and focus you need to start healing, and not only that, but the discipline to keep your thoughts on positive things.

Learn to be aware of your feelings and intuitions and trust them more: really, trust yourself! That trust is precisely what gaslighting aims to destroy because being gaslighted cuts its victims off from their self-awareness. It follows that anything that can help you to become aware of your feelings, to make decisions, and take account of your situation, is helpful.

Don't let a narcissist try to tell you that your feelings don't matter. Just because they are what we experience, rather than what we know, doesn't make them of no importance. Why would anyone who cared about you think that your feeling empty and depressed didn't matter, just because the reason for it cannot be "proved"? You can be mistaken to feel afraid when there's no danger, to give an example, but why can't that be discussed?

All human beings have intuition. This is your subconscious mind, "gut instinct," your inner spirit - there are different understandings of it and different beliefs about it. I'm not going to discuss them here; instead, I'm pointing out that we do know what intuition is in practice. We say when we look back on a natural disaster or an accident, for example, "I had a strange feeling beforehand that something wasn't right." These are the feelings I've just mentioned in the previous paragraph.

Our brains never stop working - not even when we're asleep - and gathering information about reality. This information starts being worked on before we get to the point of reasoning with it so as to work out our certainties. Just because it isn't as clear and cut-and-dried as what we can work out by reason is no reason to ignore it. Often it's an early warning or a sort of alarm that refuses to go off even when our reason has been messed with by gaslighting.

Being abused emotionally results in your becoming mentally dependent. Restoring or building your inner life and thought is helped greatly when you realize that you don't need to submit everything you do to someone else to validate it. You might object: have I not just said that you NEED to talk to other people and hear their judgments of what you share? In reality, there's no contradiction in saying you don't need to submit your decisions to others, but you need to talk to them.

The fact of talking to people about your experiences, and asking their opinions, isn't that they make the decisions for you. You can choose to accept their views or advice or not. You can decide for yourself if someone is dealing with you in good will or not. At the end of the day, you make the final decision. Even if it's wrong sometimes ... dear victim, that's not the end of the world. We all err. Just think over things again, and make a new decision. One learns from one's mistakes.

Part of not falling into useless, though understandable, feelings of shame because you've ended up in an unhappy, gaslighted state is not to take things personally. Words are said to victims, accusations made, even stupid accusations, just to hurt them. Don't take it personally. Narcissists look for and choose empathetic, sociable, nurturing types of people, such as you, to parasitize. Don't take it personally... Abusers have an ability to see and discern childhood victims who "fawn" to others, seeking love.

If that describes you, don't take it personally! Narcissists are so obsessed with themselves that their whole world is just an extension of themselves. So what they do and think is really just about them. Not you! So don't take it personally. They may be very aware, eerily aware, of some of your character traits, strengths, and weaknesses - but only in as much as they are of use to THEM or relate to them. Actually, they couldn't care less about how you think or feel, regarding those thoughts and feelings in themselves. So, don't take it personally. You must be tired of my repeating these words; however, I'm saying them so many times because that's how important they are!

It's almost a summary of many points made here, but this is an essential thing to say to yourself when you realize that you've been a victim of gaslighting: "I'm not going to let myself be a victim again. I'm going to resist the bad influences!" Refuse to accept their opinions or to be affected by their words. As I have explained, it's not very effective to challenge them openly, though you would be quite right to say calmly, "I'm sorry, I don't want to say anything more. That is a lie, and I know what the truth is." Often, the best way to do that will be simply to walk away from the argument or conversation. You won't stop a gaslighter from gaslighting if that word means "attempting to confuse you," but you are stopping the gaslighting if that means "your being confused."

Now, let me ask you some questions, and you must write down your answers. Firstly, look back on your life and ask yourself the following:

On a scale of one to ten, how badly do you think you've been affected by gaslighting? Be honest with yourself. If you've been exposed to it for a long time, very intensely, or in a hidden way, it's likely to be worse. That's not your fault. So: from one to ten, where are you?

Now you can answer the following questions:

↓

Can you think of specific occasions where you lost your temper, became muddled, or kept on trying to explain yourself to your abuser? How did you feel afterward?

_____

_____

_____

_____

_____

What practical steps can you take so that you don't end up doing these things?

Which people are you going to talk to for some direction, understanding, and unbiased advice? If you've started doing this already, list who you have talked to.

If you've hidden the worst of your abuse, start thinking about sharing your story: it's one of the best ways to get over gaslighting. You can start here.

_____

_____

_____

_____

_____

_____

What have you done, and are you going to do to calm your mind, focus on your surroundings, and be aware of your inner feelings?

_____

_____

_____

_____

_____

Have your gut feelings or instincts warned you about the person who's been abusing you? What did you sense? Did you heed the warning?

_____

_____

_____

_____

_____

Do you take things personally too often? What do you feel guilty about but know you don't have to feel responsible for?

_____

_____

_____

_____

Think of a specific resolution you need to make in your life at this point regarding your efforts to recover from gaslighting. Write it down.

_____

_____

_____

_____

_____

_____

_____

_____

_____

_____

_____

CHAPTER 12:

USEFUL WAYS TO REBUILD AND RECOVER

There are quite a few useful techniques and considerations I still need to explain to you before dealing with two very different symptoms of being gaslighted (surges of unpleasant emotions - flashbacks - and feeling unable to tell reality from delusion) in the chapters following this one.

The first is what's called the "Gray Rock" strategy. This is more of a way to handle your abuser than to handle yourself, but because it helps you to concentrate more on yourself when it works, I'm mentioning it now. Quite simply, this is to act in their presence as if you were a gray rock— hard, unchanging, not calling attention to yourself - just "there" - not moving, not making a noise. Quite safe... This is to have a calm attitude where you don't let your abuser see any fear, anger, or shock in you. You don't want to make it obvious that you'll be doing this, and it's not revenge of any sort.

You use this technique when you cannot leave your abuser for whatever reason, and so perhaps still live with or work with him or her. It can be employed when a parent has to allow a narcissistic ex-spouse to have some time with their child or children. You speak in a non-committal way, even agree outwardly with some of the nonsense you hear, while inwardly, you refuse to be bound to it. You can be pleasant but firm and just not seem very emotional.

Keep your mind on other, better things than the situation before you. Yes, it's hard at first. Don't I know! Your hands may be shaking with fear, or maybe even more with anger, and they can see the shaking. Don't worry: with a little practice, this act will become easier, and you really will be calmer and firmer.

Just resolve firmly that you will NOT LISTEN to their nonsense, even when it drones on. What you actually do when you succeed in being a "Gray Rock" is to appear to be unaffected by your gaslighter, to appear as if they have no power over you - which is the message you want to carry across. You'll be cutting off their narcissistic supply. That might encourage them to want to leave you alone.

Because narcissists and their co-dependent victims both don't see boundaries very easily, as a recovering victim, you need to set them for yourself. You may decide to speak to them only about certain issues, and you have to set these boundaries openly, unlike the previous technique. You might say to Acrid Alice that if she starts insulting you instead of talking to you, you'll stop the conversation, end the phone call, or walk away... Some people have to set up an arrangement where communication happens only through lawyers.

If you set this up, then under no circumstances do you let the abuser contact you directly. Block their phone numbers; some victims go as far as asking a friend to read any e-mail they get from their abuser. They simply forward it to them without reading it.

Now, ask yourself: how do you talk to yourself? Do you criticize yourself constantly to others or in your own thoughts? In your head, do you repeat the criticisms of your gaslighting narcissist? Learn to recognize when this happens. It's an awful thing to do to yourself. So, make a conscious effort to say to yourself - I'd recommend saying it out loud if your abuser isn't around - that the criticism is garbage, and that you aren't going to believe any of it, that you have worth, and that you are recovering from abuse.

Don't analyze yourself or the conversations you have with a narcissist too much. Although doing some thinking about it all is good... although that's what I've been guiding you to do through this workbook on gaslighting... you get to a point when you need to concentrate on healing yourself and put a distance between yourself and what is really a whole lot of rubbish. Gaslighters' word-salad isn't meant to make sense, and its only purpose is to confuse you. Granted that it is very human and apparently very logical to go over what happens to you, to try to make sense of it; but once you realize that it's gaslighting, and what kind of tactics are hidden in it, then the actual conversations, insults, faked friendliness and so on, are to be ignored quietly.

When you can calm yourself down and put a little bit of mental space between you and an abusive partner, then you can judge your own words and responses so much better. Maybe you launched a verbal attack in an attempt to defend yourself, and with some space between you and that argument, you'll be able to see why your attack wasn't a good idea, how it only invited retaliation, and what would be a better way to respond. This is with an eye to your side of things, not to what your emotional abuser said.

There are strong similarities between your situation and drug addiction recovery. One of the sometimes-overlooked ways to "detox" from abuse is not psychological as such, but physical: take care of your body! Do you get enough sleep? Make sure you do. Do you eat well? I don't mean drowning your sorrows in hamburgers and chocolate milkshakes, only to feel like a pig afterwards; I mean healthy, well-prepared food. I surely don't mean surviving on leaves, either. Just eat a good, balanced diet, and you'll feel better. Then, when you do feel better, treat yourself to a chocolate milkshake on one sunny day— just one. Then carry on with your walk in the sun. You need to get enough exercise. Again, if you're not in good shape, it doesn't make sense to start weightlifting as if for a competition—just some stretching exercise, some walking, maybe some sit-ups. Once you feel better physically in the future, you could start with the dumbbells... Obviously, taking too many pain killers, or drinking alcohol alone on your own when you feel bad, are no good for anyone.

Talking to people you can trust is an important part of recovery from gaslighting. There don't have to be many of them, but they do need to have some sympathy or empathy, some wisdom to guide you, and not have their own ax to grind. Professional help has already been mentioned as an excellent solution. The tactics of gaslighting require that you be isolated from other people, unprotected and alone, so part of your overcoming it is to connect to others. Unsympathetic, gaslighted family members will not give you any help, at least not with mammoth-sized wool pulled over their eyes!

You need to hear the truth from them, so they must be really truthful with you. Some people think that a sort of syrupy sympathy given to you, in which they tell you what you want to hear, is loving. It isn't. Perhaps you need to hear that this person you've married to or been with for some time doesn't love you: because although you realize that deep down, you're still struggling to accept it. Perhaps you need to see that you fell in love with the bond you formed with them, the beautiful idea, not their ugly personality and attitudes.

People you can trust will be able to back you up and help you see when you do have a right to feel as you do, that you have reasons to want to leave or distance yourself from this person, that you have been gaslighted! You will feel so much better and think so much more clearly.

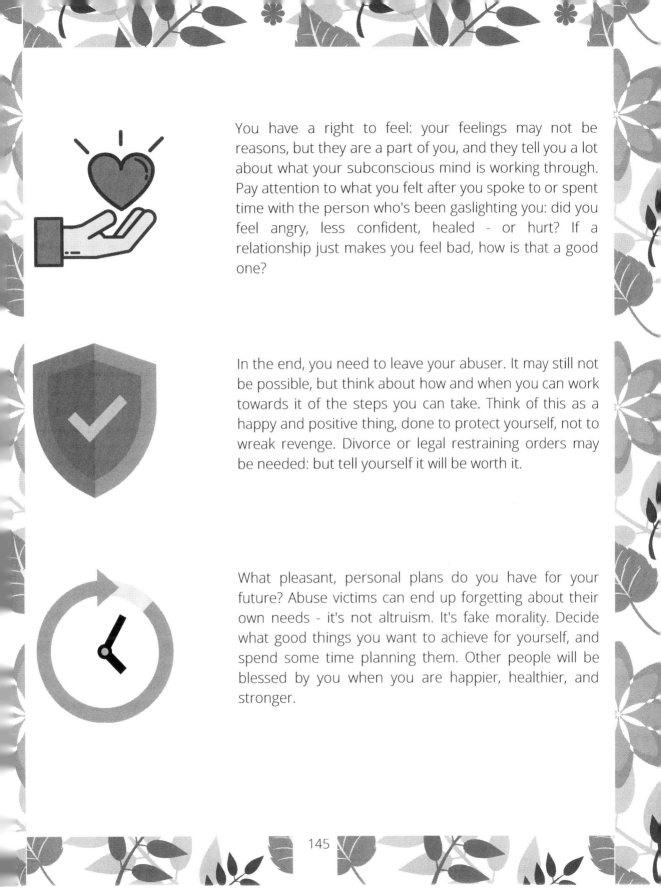

You have a right to feel: your feelings may not be reasons, but they are a part of you, and they tell you a lot about what your subconscious mind is working through. Pay attention to what you felt after you spoke to or spent time with the person who's been gaslighting you: did you feel angry, less confident, healed - or hurt? If a relationship just makes you feel bad, how is that a good one?

In the end, you need to leave your abuser. It may still not be possible, but think about how and when you can work towards it of the steps you can take. Think of this as a happy and positive thing, done to protect yourself, not to wreak revenge. Divorce or legal restraining orders may be needed: but tell yourself it will be worth it.

What pleasant, personal plans do you have for your future? Abuse victims can end up forgetting about their own needs - it's not altruism. It's fake morality. Decide what good things you want to achieve for yourself, and spend some time planning them. Other people will be blessed by you when you are happier, healthier, and stronger.

Think of the "gray rock" strategy, and if you are in a situation where you need to do this, describe what you are going to be like. What will your actions and emotions be? What will you say and not say?

✎ _____

_____

_____

_____

_____

_____

Write down any specific boundaries you need to set with your abuser. Be specific, i.e., only one parental visit per month to his/her child.

✎ _____

_____

_____

_____

_____

_____

_____

Do you catch yourself over-analyzing? When do you do this; in what situations? And what are you going to say to yourself to resist this urge? Write it down...

Look after your body! What are you going to do? Don't promise yourself the earth; just some practical, healthy behavior. Put your thoughts down hereafter.

Who are you going to talk to, or who do you talk to already, whom you can trust? Whose words can you trust to be true but also kind?

_____

_____

_____

_____

_____

Finally, what about those happy, pleasant plans for your future? What would you really like to do that is possible and achievable? Write about it here, brainstorm if you like (remember that from your preparation at the beginning of this workbook).

_____

_____

_____

_____

_____

_____

CHAPTER 13:

A NARCISSIST HAS NO POWER OVER YOU WHEN YOU STOP FLASHBACKS

Nightmares, depression, lack of social confidence, problems with forgetting facts and sequences, flashbacks and emotional flare-ups, eating too much or not wanting to eat at all, using alcohol and drugs unwisely and in excess, thoughts of suicide... all these and more are things that victims of gaslighting and any form of emotional abuse can suffer, or be tempted to do. There are many ways to overcome them, of which I've mentioned several, but for now, let's focus on flashbacks. Flashbacks have a particularly strong influence over victims, or I could say, are a sign of a strong, negative influence over victims.

Seen from either point of view, they are a serious problem - a chain of thoughts, usually negative, not rational, driven by emotions out of control, which spirals deeper and deeper. Another form starts suddenly, and is triggered by a sudden, unexpected stimulus, then dies down slowly. It's not less serious: all of us have heard of wounded, shell-shocked soldiers who dive for cover when they hear even the snap of a twig, for example.

Victims of emotional abuse tend to experience a long, spiraling chain of thoughts sparked by a surge of negative emotion. In all cases, working on controlling these emotional flashbacks is a way to break the power of the trauma another person or situation has caused you. You don't need to crush these emotions, and you can't just toss them into a mental rubbish bin; you need to understand them, face them, and use the right techniques to control them... and then you'll start to overcome flashbacks.

The difference between emotional flashbacks and other types is that you don't normally know what triggered them, e.g., there is no snapping stick to make you think of a hidden enemy or booby-trap. They are not the result of one sudden, quick trauma: in other words, not like being beaten up by a couple of thugs on a lonely road at night and having a panic attack a month later when two men come around the corner suddenly in broad daylight.

Being gaslighted for years will hurt you mentally and cause countless episodes with emotions of anger, fear, shame, confusion, and frustration. You will find yourself re-living these feelings suddenly, but it won't be in the presence of your abuser (that would be a normal, healthy response to aggression or lying...), nor will it even be when you see or experience something that reminds you of him or her. They will just come out of the blue. You probably know just what I mean. Don't worry if you have some slightly different experiences: maybe your flood of emotions comes with a picture of a supermarket you used to shop at when you were still living with the partner who gaslighted you, and you wonder why you remember the supermarket. Really, it doesn't matter - the solution lies in the same.

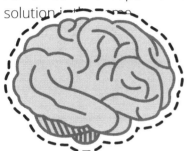

The solution lies very much in the brain and with your feelings. Let me explain: your emotional flashbacking is a memory of how you FELT when you were at your worst. How did you feel when you thought you were going crazy and every attempt you ever made to explain yourself, resolve the situation with your abuser ended in confusion, denial, and insults?

How did you feel when you were losing your memory when you were threatened and lied to and knew that you were being controlled against your will? Pretty awful, not so? These feelings are what you remember, and your brain has tried to hide the deepest and most unpleasant of them. Unfortunately, that doesn't work for long, and they re-surface.

Lesson number one: realize that you suffer from emotional flashbacks! What a relief to know that you aren't crazy. Yes, you've been abused, but if you know what happens to you and can recognize that you are starting an emotional flashback, that's the beginning of control. Let me illustrate it with a metaphorical example: once you know that those horrid little brown grains you find in the storeroom in the morning are mouse droppings, then you've identified the problem. You had wondered if it were cockroaches, you'd sprayed insecticide, you'd thought of bats in the ceiling and dreaded trying to open it up... Yes, now you have to get mousetraps and to keep the door open at night so the cats can get in, but no longer will you be feeling frustrated and angry, wondering what the matter is. When you can say to yourself, "This is a flashback!" you'll have it in your sights.

So - suppose you are having a flashback, and now you know it. The next thing is to look at what kind of stresses you are experiencing. Although you might not have a particular trigger, emotional flashbacks do happen when you are feeling stressed. Your brain remembers your past feelings of stress and helplessness, associates it with the feelings of stress and being overwhelmed that are in your present situation, in that minute, puts them together, adding the past feelings to your present experience... and - pow!

You might say, "How stupid!" but the brain is actually meaning to help you overcome this. Imagine it was a feeling of helplessness and fear, felt over a long time when you lived in the jungle, that there might be a giant python hiding in the greenery... and so making you very quiet and hyper-vigilant. Then later, in any stressful situation, your brain recalls it; so that you can be extra-quiet and hyper-vigilant, presumably because "danger" is like a python.

It's your animal brain at work, and the fact that you also jump instantly out of the way of a car hurtling down the street, rather than thinking about its course, is thanks to that part of your brain. However, emotional stress and confusion of your higher reason are a very different sort of danger than pythons or speeding automobiles!

You have an "animal brain"; and also an "angel's brain," as I like to call it, the part that operates in pure reason and transcends time. It's this part of you that you are going to use to look at your emotions wisely and logically: coldly when you need to use cold logic, or with compassion when it comes to the need to be kind to yourself, rather than punish yourself for what happened to you as an innocent victim, in the past.

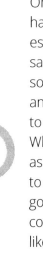

One of the keys to overcoming negative emotions is to work against the harm they do to your mind and body. Just think and do the opposite, especially when one starts to happen to you. You might hear a voice saying, "You're ugly and useless at social interactions!" It might be something your parents didn't actually say but implied all the same. At any rate, it's not you saying this: that little, internal critic is not you! So say to yourself that it's really a flashback and that flashbacks have a cure.

Why not make yourself a slogan or motto to repeat to yourself? This is not as much a mantra to calm you as it is a statement of fact with the intent to help you internalize a healthy, balanced mindset. Try saying, "I'm not going to dwell on this sadness: I'm learning to handle stress by concentrating on positive things!" Then start thinking of something you like.

Do all the things I've mentioned in previous chapters to look after yourself: eat well, sleep enough, be in the company of some good people, pray and meditate, make plans for things you find meaningful and happy, play happy or calm music, etcetera. If you've just had an argument with someone, maybe you need to apologize if that's what's called for. Maybe you need to go for a walk to clear your head; smell the flowers, pat a dog, look at the pretty girls in the street/handsome boys in the park, look at the fancy Georgian houses along the road on the way back... I think I've given you enough examples. These are things you probably do anyway, but I'm asking you to do them quite deliberately when you sense that you're becoming too stressed. As if you could say, "My stress barometer has risen to seven out of ten! I need a break to get it down." Later you can say, "Now I'm at four. Much better! I can handle life when it's at four, but let me see if I can't reduce it a little more." You want to be able to realize that flashbacks happen to you really badly when your level is seven or higher, only occasionally when it's at four to six, and not at all when it's lower. You don't have to calibrate yourself quite like this - don't despair! - all I mean is that you are looking to develop an awareness of yourself and your states of mind.

Now, to become aware of your feelings and states of mind, you need to listen to the inner voice that runs in your head, especially when you have a flashback. Also, there may be a picture or vivid memory which is recalled. They will be negative, it goes without saying, and unpleasant for you. However, don't try to avoid them: examine them. What does the voice say? Who is saying that: you or someone else? What do you see? Where is it? Don't you realize that you can talk to yourself in different words and make yourself see other pictures?

When these flashbacks come, do they make you tense, curl up, and make you breathe faster? What about trying to breathe deeply and more slowly and lying flat on your back with your arms stretched over your head?

When you become more aware of your moods and your level of stress, you'll start to develop the skills to defuse the stress bombs before they explode. You might feel warning signs or see some kind of trigger in your imagination. Once you can sense the danger, you can choose how to react; most often, the best reaction is not to react and to wait for a while, by which time the moods and emotions will have faded or passed.

Try leaving the place where you are and go for a walk; try stopping the work you've been doing and start another task. You literally have to try not to let yourself feel the emotions as they well up inside you. When you sense that you have a desire to shout and lash out at the thought of someone, try to do something physical that is different and less 'exciting,' Maybe you can wash the dishes; maybe eat lunch!

If you do find the emotions of a flashback too intense to fight against, and you ended up bursting into tears, for example... rather than feeling bad about your outburst, try to think about what you experienced.

Once a flashback has gone, it is good to analyze it. You can write about why you felt as you did. The thing with emotions is that they come in many different "flavors" and "colors," and you need to be aware of these. If you are a man reading this, you may find this rather odd to accept, and many women also struggle with this. Really, truly, we are never just "sad," "angry," "calm," or "afraid." So, to illustrate, we can be angry about a beloved family member doing something truly horrible to someone else, with tears running down our cheeks. That's angry, sad, disappointed, shocked, and pleading for an explanation, all in one. When you can write something like this down, you can see that you're not just "having an emotional reaction to anger," but that you are deeply disappointed in them; maybe you will see that you've become dependent on them, and put that person on a pedestal without ceasing to like them or have affection for them, you need to have more confidence in yourself. A counselor or therapist is a tremendous help in coming to be more aware of your emotions and finding the way to root them in reality.

One of the ways to understand emotional flashbacks is to be able to classify them. As a victim of gaslighting, they are more likely to be of sadness and fear than of anger or over-excitement. However, you could be harboring a lot of anger towards the person who gaslighted you or is still doing it to you. Are you, or were you, being baited to lose your temper, thereby demonstrating to both of you that you were out of control? You can notice that your feelings of anger have a lot of fear and frustration underlying them: fear of losing the little control of your life you were allowed to have by your abuser; the frustration of never being understood - no matter how much you tried to explain yourself to him or her, or to the other people your abuser converted into their "flying monkeys."

Someone who mistakenly devoted himself or herself for a long time to a narcissistic gaslighter will know, perhaps, that he or she suffers emotional flashbacks of intense sadness. If that victim examines these feelings, then the victim may come to see that more than sadness, they suffer a feeling of having wasted so much of their lives on their abuser, yet contrasted with a desperate longing to experience the feelings of joy they had when the relationship first began. Others may see that their sadness is mixed with deep shame, that actually they are more ashamed of themselves for getting into the state they have than they are sad about leaving an abusive relationship.

Other victims are overwhelmed by feelings of fear; they might actually be feeling fear mixed with avoidance and the shame of not having achieved the goals they set for themselves. Some feel fear but don't want to think, so try to do too many things to stop thinking about their pain. Yes, recovery from any kind of flashback does involve looking at uncomfortable realities - but I repeat, it's worth it! If you start to see what is underlying your flashbacks, you are starting to see reality; and as you do so, the flashbacks will lose their power... which is the power your gaslighting abuser has wielded over you. Don't give up! Failure in one situation is not the end. Learn to manage yourself, and accept that it takes practice.

I want to take you back to the second chapter of this book, where we looked at how you can be vulnerable to narcissistic personalities, to the types who gaslight others because of their childhood experiences. Once you begin to understand your feelings and the way they manifested in emotional flashbacks, you should be able to see how the flashbacks relate to emotions you felt as a child, or at least, long ago. Your brain has memorized your traumatic experiences as feelings and physical stress-responses of your body, forgetting much of the painful, confusing facts.

Once you can understand your past better and be more aware of what your flashbacks remind you of, you will heal, and the flashback episodes will decrease. Of course, you need to make an effort to do this, to train your mind to think differently and better: remember that time did not heal everything because your mind was suppressing your earlier pain, rather than confronting and accepting what actually happened.

Some things to consider here are potential problems for you precisely because of your inner trauma and suppression, on top of the harm you have suffered later in life by being gaslighted. Painful memories are... painful. This sounds obvious, but some people are very reluctant and quite frightened of trying to re-live them. However, you need to do it, especially to feel sad about what happened. Sadness, rather than avoidance, is a way to acknowledge that something was bad and accept that it happened. After you let yourself feel the sadness, you can realize that the abuse was in the past and that now you are in the present, with an opportunity to move on from your past.

A compassionate and helpful listener, especially a professional, can help you to feel a certain amount of grief as you look over your emotions and the situations they came from.

Another problem comes from the same effort recovering victims must make to re-live and analyze their experiences: you may feel resistance as anger and feel as if your therapist, friend, or relative who is supposed to be helping you, is invading your mind, judging you, or trying to manipulate you. Literally, he or she has taken the place of a childhood figure of authority, perhaps one who neglected or abused you; or even more likely, one whom you blame for not protecting you enough or helping you to live with the parent who did neglect or abuse you. You may find yourself blaming your therapist or saying that your attempts to recover from gaslighting aren't working!

A compassionate and helpful listener will not lose his or her temper with you - but will ask you to stop, think about what is happening, and show you that you need to understand where this is coming from: your "animal brain" is trying to protect your inner self, your core, but it's projecting a false picture. The animal brain isn't logical.

If this happens, you will need to look after yourself more carefully than ever to reduce your stress levels and examine your emotional response. Repeat the phrases you use to stay positive every day. Don't stop any of the good practices you began, and understand that this feeling of resistance does not come from the behavior of the person who's helping you and that it's not your fault. Just don't accept it as real, though!

If you can work through these projected emotions and see them for what they are, you should feel a lot better, and your flashbacks should also reduce. Likewise, if you work on your flashbacks, your feelings of animosity to your counselor or other confidants should reduce as well.

In time, with patience and effort, your emotional flashbacks should stop. Really, they are so much a sign of unhealed wounds that you need to set yourself the goal of not having them anymore.

So many other things will work out better for you when you've overcome them; you will have got your revenge on the narcissist who gaslighted you, for one! Your living well is, as they say, the best form of revenge, rather than playing a childish, destructive tit-for-tat game.

You will no longer be seeing the world through mud-stained glasses because flashbacks come from a state of mind that warps and clouds all of your perceptions.

Think about the way you feel when an emotional flashback hits you: what is the main emotion you feel?

_____
_____
_____
_____
_____

Now, I want you to describe all the ways in which you feel that emotion and any other emotions that may be mixed with it. Use at least ten describing words.

_____
_____
_____
_____
_____

What negative, repetitive things does your "inner critic" say to you?

_____

_____

_____

_____

_____

I would like you to look at the past week, seven days. On a scale from one to ten, how would you rate your average stress level on each day? It's subjective: don't worry about the measurement too much, but it's still important to try to describe it with a number. Can you name any individual experiences, times, or situations that stand out for being more or less stressful?

Sunday   Monday   Tuesday   Wednesday

Thursday   Friday   Saturday

What things can you do to look after yourself better?

_____

_____

_____

_____

_____

What things are you doing already to take care of yourself?

_____

_____

_____

_____

_____

Going back to your childhood: what memories or feelings can you remember from then that are the same or like the feelings and the sensations you get when you have flashbacks?

_____

_____

_____

_____

_____

Do you ever find yourself becoming angry with or hurt by a person you're trying to talk to about your flashbacks? Especially if he or she is a counselor or psychologist?

_____

_____

_____

_____

_____

What exactly are those feelings? Try to describe them here:

_____

_____

_____

_____

_____

_____

I want you to talk to them about these feelings. Don't be ashamed: if he or she isn't a professional, explain that you know why it's happening; let them hear and read the end of this chapter, and let them know that it mustn't be taken personally, and assure them that you don't want these reactions, but they're just part of healing yourself. Write what you want to say:

_____

_____

_____

_____

_____

_____

What slogans or catchphrases can you use for yourself every day to act against your inner critic? What ones can you say to yourself whenever you feel that you're starting to have a flashback or are in danger of drifting into one?

✒ _____

_____

_____

_____

What thoughts do you have during flashbacks that cloud or confuse you about decisions you need to make or interfere with the goals of your life? After reading this chapter, can you see how stopping emotional flashbacks will help you to make and attain them?

✒ _____

_____

_____

_____

_____

CHAPTER 14:

HOW TO KEEP YOUR SENSE OF REALITY

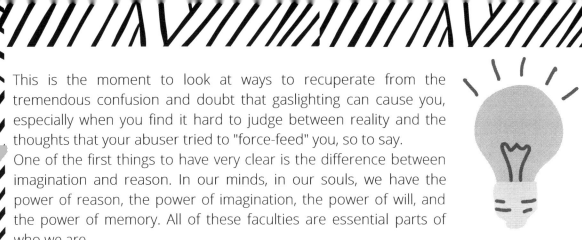

This is the moment to look at ways to recuperate from the tremendous confusion and doubt that gaslighting can cause you, especially when you find it hard to judge between reality and the thoughts that your abuser tried to "force-feed" you, so to say.

One of the first things to have very clear is the difference between imagination and reason. In our minds, in our souls, we have the power of reason, the power of imagination, the power of will, and the power of memory. All of these faculties are essential parts of who we are.

The imagination helps our will to be motivated to do or think something, or not to do it; it helps us to dream of possibilities and helps to picture our memories in bright colors. However, it isn't a higher power than is our reason, or will, or memory. What can happen, however, is that when we are traumatized or confused, the imagination can run amok. We can all remember what it's done in our dreams when we've been enraged, or suffered an accident, when we were tiny children and deeply afraid or over-excited, or perhaps during an unfortunate experience with drugs or alcohol.

As a victim of narcissistic abuse, or any abuse involving some sort of gaslighting, you've been confused deliberately, sometimes subtly, sometimes openly, and maybe for a long time. Your imagination will have been targeted and made to run over your reason, to deny your memories, to force your will to accept what it was trying to resist. Flashbacks are a particular case of the imagination running wild and taking over for a short time. Recovery is going to be a process of using your mind to control and guide your imagination properly again and using your memory as well to correct it.

Imagination isn't bad; some people don't use it often enough. However, most of us who tend to use it too much need to learn these controlling skills to attain peace of mind and deal with other people more happily and more justly.

Your memory is also a wonderful faculty, but as with any human ability, it can also be disturbed and affected by gaslighting. It isn't one hundred percent accurate - ask any two people to remember the same event - and it wasn't meant to be. Even though some victims have a tendency to dwell on all the unpleasant memories of their abuse and fall into depression, others tend to forget past abuse too easily, especially when they've left an abusive relationship and are struggling to adapt to a new way of life.

Perhaps they've formed trauma bonds with an abusive family member or intimate partner and feel a mistaken devotion to that person even after being badly treated and managing to distance themselves or have no contact. Recall the chapter on childhood and abusive treatment...

Perhaps you went through a bad period in your life when you were at school. For example, you were lonely, bullied, struggled with spelling and grammar, were criticized by some teachers, and made over-sensitive to that criticism. Now in later adult life, you find nevertheless that you have a lot of good memories: the few friends you did make, the school holiday you went on where you saw the Grand Canyon, the silly behavior of the History teacher that you can laugh at now.

Perhaps you can see that, though not perfect, you actually had a good education in some areas. This is a sort of "selective amnesia," a chosen forgetfulness of your memory, which has toned down the unpleasant parts (after all, they're dead and gone...) and kept fully open your access to the better ones. This is a positive thing, and it's why I'm saying that your memory isn't meant to be a one-hundred-percent accurate recall. I mean, you can still remember the bad things and be warned by them or learn from them, but with time they have faded.

However, if you've been abused emotionally or physically, and it is ongoing, or in the recent past, it's not a good thing to start seeing things through "rose-tinted spectacles." The minds - the memories - of some victims start doing this when there is still damage to be repaired and action to be taken. How would you know this if it's the case with you? Well, do you find yourself looking back at the honeymoon phase, symbolic or actual, that you had with the person who abused you and feel sad? Do you find yourself saying and feeling, "I still love her/him..."? Do you find yourself telling people only the petty, little incidents of your sufferings, hiding the most shocking ones? Or do you admit the incidents of abuse but feel somewhat ashamed to have endured them - maybe making excuses for your abuser regarding his or her behavior you suffered from? All these are signs of your memory, imagination, and will being cut off from your reason, from the truth. People who have been gaslighted are more likely to do this than victims of other types of abuse. You aren't stupid - but you are a victim. Yet this shows how much you need to root yourself back into the good soil of reasonable, logical care of yourself and taking reasonable steps to protect your well-being!

One of the best tools to help you has already been mentioned in Chapter Eleven: the notes you made before and during reading this workbook! Here, you have written accurate notes of what happened to you, what was said to you, and what you did and said. These are what you can go back to when you feel tempted to say that you've over-reacted to the person who you were upset by and that you are the stupid one; when you try to remember something about it in a given moment - but your mind seems to go blank. These notes are your guide to keeping in touch with reality. Reality is the truth: yes, it may hurt sometimes, but it always heals.

Nightmares, depression, lack of social confidence, problems with forgetting facts and sequences, flashbacks, and emotional flare-ups can all dog people for a long time after abuse if they don't get help. You can speed up your recovery from all of these and others when you can focus your mind on reality - both the reality of what you suffered and the reality of the present. You are going to make a conscious effort to find out, hold onto and believe the reality of your life to guide you along the path of healing from gaslighting.

Isn't it better just to stop thinking about the past and forget it all? In a moment of experiencing a flashback, or when you suddenly find yourself going down a chain of negative thoughts in your mind, indeed, it is a good thing to make an effort to stop thinking these thoughts at once. You can make a positive affirmation to yourself.

So if you find yourself saying, for instance, something like: "I've wasted the last fifteen years of my life with Simon Greenalgey. I could have had a child, but he didn't want children. Now it's too late... I've lost most of my friends. I'm too tired and worn out to make new friends... No one's ever going to love me. I'm going to spend the rest of my life as a lonely old divorcée..." you can stop yourself. Say, "No! I'm a survivor. I've managed to see the light and break free. There's a world full of people to love, and I'm going to find the good in them. I have life; I have hope. There is a future!"

Well and good. Yet the fact is that you were abused, and the effects can't just be wished away. Parts of your mind are literally attacking you, and you need to identify them and shine the light there... So, you have your notes about your abuse. In these, you can see why you had to leave if you've left this person. Or, you can see what's been done to you and what you still have to manage if you can't leave this person or have left but need to have some limited contact. Because our memories try to avoid thinking on the most hideous incidents of abuse and give us "selective amnesia," I want you to do the following right after this paragraph: write down all the reasons why you left this person if you have, and all the worst incidents; or all the reasons why you have to manage them, all the worst incidents that gave and give you a reason to keep yourself distant from them emotionally, to leave them in the future. Don't write just one or two: come on, there must be eight, ten, fifteen of them... Use your existing notes to help you!

I'm keeping N. at a distance, and I have to protect myself because... or I had to leave N. because...

_____

_____

_____

_____

_____

_____

_____

_____

_____

_____

I ask you to do this because I'm aware that everyone has SOME good in them; I know that leaving someone, perhaps moving away to a place you don't know or haven't been living in for a long time, puts a strain on anyone. As for continuing to live with someone who is so difficult, who you are going to have to manage without their realizing quite what you are doing... that's even harder. So it's odd but understandable that you may get temptations to go back; start hoping that you can manage them with a little more love and understanding... Yet you absolutely cannot go back to the state you were in! Look at these reasons you have written, and realize that a narcissist is not the reason you managed to survive that awful time of your life! He or she is the principal reason for your suffering from then till now!

This is really true when you start to realize how little love and encouragement you've had. It's quite likely that was so when you were a child. You need to learn how to encourage yourself and acknowledge what you've got and what you've achieved. You yourself need to care for, love, and affirm yourself. Don't look for this affirmation and support from your abuser. That person may have "love-bombed" you once or twice, but don't you see that it was only to get something from you? That isn't love.

I'm not telling you to wallow in all the bad experiences you had or to be negative. I'm telling you to protect yourself from the irrational thoughts you may find floating about in your head. Also, I'm giving you this advice to protect yourself, if your abuser should decide that he or she has to get you back; or decides that he or she wants you again, after having thrown you in their mental "trash can"!

Relationship counselors call it "hoovering" sometimes. This is when a narcissist leaves a victim, usually because he or she's found a new one, and then when that doesn't go according to plan, they decide that they want the previous victim back again. Like throwing dirt on the carpet, then sucking it up again with a vacuum cleaner... Badly confused, unloved victims can see this as a sign that they were loved, after all, or perhaps, that after not being loved well the first time, their former abuser will start loving them better the second time around. This is always, inevitably, wrong!! Be warned... and if he or she comes back with an over-sized bunch of expensive roses or the offer of a candle-lit supper he or she went to the utmost lengths to prepare... say: "Thank you; that looks/sounds very nice, but I'm really not interested in changing my life. I'm fine as I am." And go off find your gaslighting-recovery workbook, and read about all the reasons why you are doing very well to stay away from that person!

Staying away, if you can do it, is staying away mentally. That would be by having no phone calls from that person, blocking them from your social media, and not looking at theirs. You don't want to be tearing your heart out that Poisoning Pete seems to be enjoying life with his updated model of a female companion. Is it real, anyway? Is it not just a "love-bombing" phase that will end just as surely as yours did? You may be tempted to look at the approving comments by other people and doubt yourself, feel inferior. It doesn't matter what they think: reading it is actually gaslighting you! You know what Poisoning Pete is capable of because you married him and stayed five years with him, let's say. None of them have! If you had to have some kind of contact with him regarding a divorce settlement or parental obligations, etcetera, it might be the best arrangement to have contact only through a lawyer.

How many reasons did you write about? Keep it private, and don't flinch from telling your story as it was, from giving your reasons and showing your thoughts to yourself. At this point, recalling and spelling out what happened, how you felt (feelings are not irrelevant), you may realize that one of your deepest feelings after abuse is SHAME. You feel that you've failed to protect yourself, that you should have been able to manage your life, that you've failed totally... and, or, you feel so damaged that nobody will ever love or want you again. To get better, you have to decide to overcome this feeling, choose to have hope, and aim for something.

What do you want your life to be? You are allowed to hope, you know! Any activity that projects you into the future but that you can work at today, anything that makes you feel better, is positively recommended. If you still live with the person who was gaslighting you - don't, please don't, say to yourself that you can't start thinking about the future until you've left that relationship! In your own mind and heart, you need to start planning your future life now, just as all healthy, happy people do, just as most people do, happy or not. In this way, you can use what you wrote about how you felt and suffered as a starting point to write about how you want to feel and what you want to do. You have a right to be happy and feel inner peace, but if you keep shaming yourself inside, that can't happen. As I say, don't love other people and hate yourself: it's not actually possible. Love your neighbor as yourself!

Try this exercise: what would you tell someone else who had exactly the same experience of abuse as you? What kind of advice would you give them? By doing this, you are actually putting yourself back in your own shoes, connecting yourself back to reality. Would you really say, "Well, that's just the way it is? You just have to accept it and try not to feel sorry for yourself?" More than just telling them you do feel sorry for them, what practical advice would you give them, and what would you recommend that they did? You would be compassionate to someone you knew and loved if they needed you. Connecting to reality after gaslighting is a way of having compassion for yourself because a narcissist forced an illusion onto you and denied your reality; reality is the truth we need to look after ourselves with, and to be able to look after others.

Here are some more focusing questions for you:

What kind of things have you found yourself imagining about your life that are unreal, unpleasant, too negative, or downright silly? Don't feel bad: imagination can often be crazy. Write them down honestly, and don't skip the embarrassing details.

_____

_____

_____

_____

_____

_____

_____

_____

What good things or happy memories do you have of the person who abused you? How do they make you feel now?

_____

_____

_____

_____

_____

Are these happy memories things that actually happened, or were they just promises made or conjured feelings? Does your reason tell you that a lot of this wasn't actually of the person you were with but was about you?

_____

_____

_____

_____

_____

_____

Do you feel ashamed of yourself? Describe your shameful feelings. Why are you ashamed?

_____

_____

_____

_____

_____

Depression, problems with sleeping too much or too little, flashbacks, lacking confidence before other people, nightmares, emotional flare-ups and outbursts, loss of appetite or binge-eating, forgetfulness, problems with concentrating... All are problems gaslighting can cause in victims. Which of these do you, have you suffered from? Any other problems? Write them down.

_____

_____

_____

_____

_____

Go back and look at what you wrote about your happy memories and any feelings of having loved and lost someone you may be aware of. Now, look at the last two questions and your answers there. How does it all add up? Where did having this relationship leave you?

_____

_____

_____

_____

_____

Let's do something happier: use your imagination and think of what good things you'd like to happen in the future. Picture and describe them.

_____

_____

_____

_____

_____

_____

CHAPTER 15:

HOW A GASLIGHTER WILL REACT WHEN YOU RESIST

How will someone who's been gaslighting you react when you start to resist? Above all, how will he or she behave if you break the news to them that you are leaving when you've been in an intimate relationship with a narcissist?

Well, I must be honest and say: "Very badly." The truth is that facing this challenge is one of the difficult things you have to do to defend your peace of mind. Not only have you had to suffer from their usual bad behavior, but when they start to lose control over you - especially if you announce that you're leaving - they will behave worse than before.

In the same way you are learning to resist your negative mental brainwashing from the past, by acting logically and positively from within your thoughts and emotions, you will also have to resist your abuser's antagonism coming from outside. However: don't despair; don't think of this as a totally new battle you need to fight. It is part of the same effort you've been making already.

Before explaining why this happens and what you must prepare yourself for, I want to answer a question asked by many: Do you tell a gaslighter that he is "a gaslighter"? Do you say to a narcissist that she is "a narcissist"?

No! What are you thinking to accomplish by doing so? To make them see the error of their ways? All that has been explained to you in this workbook, and so many other writings by psychologists, make it clear that the "Cluster B Personalities," as they are referred to, don't feel any kind of responsibility or remorse. They refuse to see their faults. They are also hypersensitive to any criticism, and accusing someone by labeling them with these terms is hardly giving them a compliment, is it? Are you still thinking that you have to find a sufficiently good reason to explain why you are resisting their gaslighting tactics, to justify your leaving them, or at least, no longer co-operating? Forget it.

You must make your own decision and follow through with it. Another thing to remember is that these types of people love playing the victim: you labeling them as a gaslighter is simply going to spur them into trying to convince everyone, you included if possible, that they are the victim... and you, the abuser! You don't want to give information to people with these kinds of personalities: they see information as a weapon to attack you with, not as the means to find the truth.

I can't stop gaslighters from buying this or other books on gaslighting. I can advise you to keep this workbook very secret from your abuser and tell you that you have no reason to feel guilty about doing so. You need to recover and look after your inner thoughts and yourself. If you can leave and have decided to do so, don't think that you are morally obliged to announce it with a blast of steel trumpets. There is no goodwill in a narcissistic personality to consider, that obliges you to behave as you would, openly, with a normal person.

The reaction of your abuser to you resisting their efforts to confuse and weaken your beliefs, to make you reject your feelings, has to be understood as the manifestation of what sort of a person he or she is. This is their inner person, as previous chapters and your notes have shown: "Cass Geistlichter" doesn't care about you as a person; he has no empathy. He thinks he's the best, the cleverest, the most unrecognized man in the world. He feels envy and is deeply competitive. He's terribly sensitive to any criticism and so becomes violently protective of what he sees as being his rights. Anything that might go wrong in his business, intimate relationship, or family is YOUR fault. He tries his utmost to believe he is always right, always. He will never look back over his day and ask himself if he did the right thing because whenever he goes where he wants to, he thinks he's where he should be all the time. When he's not... it must be someone else's fault. He doesn't see a need to understand himself: he may feel there's something "other" lurking inside him, but he's in no mood to open a can of worms, and it's far easier to convince himself that he knows himself perfectly.

Cass Geistlichter is an actor in his own play: the hero and in the audience, all at once. He hates even the thought of being weak or vulnerable, and so he seeks power all the time. He's proud, haughty, and sneers very often. He enjoys harming and abusing you because it makes him look stronger and better than you. And he's a CHILD. Deep down, despite his memory and intelligence being those of an adult, he's a sulking, self-centered, spoiled child!

If this person, or his female equivalent, senses that you've changed, that you've seen through his actor's mask, that you're resisting, he will strike back. If a country goes to war, the army has to plan for it and to do so, they have to look at what material and personnel they have and at what they know about their enemy. Victim of gaslighting: do the same! I'm not advising you to go to war in the sense of attacking your abuser in the same way he or she attacked you because you can see by now that this doesn't work. The illustration here is that you must prepare for the conflict by understanding your abuser. You must know what you can expect.

Gaslighters are people who fear rejection. They do realize that their actions would cause other people to reject them, I believe. This is exactly one of their reasons for trying to make you passive and dependent on them so that you find it harder to resist. It's just as true to say, in contrast, that a gaslighter is dependent on you! Also, they are highly suspicious of others, knowing that many people (really, almost everyone) do not have the sky-high opinion of them that they think they deserve. Their personality traits make them defensive, and their arrogant lack of concern for others makes attacking their best form of defense. They don't have a clear idea of their behavior having any effects, and if you should announce that you're going to leave or that you have, it will be seen as an unprovoked attack.

So how will they react badly? They will react with fear and frenzy if they are very dependent on you. They always wanted you to take all their insults personally, just as they will take your resistance to them as a personal insult. They will usually attack.

I have to distinguish the types of possible reactions of a gaslighter rejected: the attack is a reaction of a person who is dependent on, who still wants his or her victim. Another possibility is that the victim is still "narcissistic supply," in other words, the victim still gives power, validation, and service to the abuser, but the abuser will try to play a game of false acceptance. He or she might say something like, "Oh, so you're leaving me. Here's a suitcase for you." And they just walk away. Obviously, this is playing another game. He or she is trying to surprise you, perhaps sensing that you were braced for an attack and hoping maybe their false surrender will unnerve you. They may also hope that that you're still bonded to them in trauma and that you're going to start missing them and grieving once the familiar patterns of your life suddenly end. If you feel this way too, look at the advice in earlier chapters, and don't fall for it! You've actually had a lucky escape (for now, at least: your abuser may change tactics).

There may be another reason for an abuser to react with indifference: he or she might have been at the point of rejecting you! A male gaslighter who's been unfaithful to his wife for some time, for example, may have found her "replacement." If she's the one who asks for a divorce, he takes advantage to make it look as if he's the deserted one! A female gaslighter who reacts unexpectedly calmly is, I think, even more likely to have her male partner's "replacement" all lined up...

This does not exclude the possibility of an abuser who is rejecting a victim, nevertheless staging a furious reaction. The difference is that it is "staged." He or she will probably recover surprisingly quickly because it wasn't a real sense of loss.

However, most gaslighters will feel totally betrayed and will be really angered, hurt, and panic. The more immature he or she is inside, the worse the feeling will be. I can't "sugar-coat" this bitter pill...

...The abuser is likely to do some or many of the following: insult you, de-humanize you, say the worst, most personal things they can think of, use everything they know about your weaknesses to exploit you;

they'll make out the best thing you ever did for them was an attempt to hate them, they'll try to punish you as if you were a child, to destroy anything they know or think you like; they'll try to use other people to hurt you, will tell lies about you to them.

They might threaten or stalk you. Physical violence happens in some cases - especially if your abuser has resorted to physical aggression before.

You need to plan what you will do. If you cannot leave the partner, colleague, or family member who gaslights you, then you need to make your resistance a covert operation. Using the "gray rock technique" would be recommended, though once a narcissist senses your resistance, you will have to resist more openly. Just do it as calmly as possible.

If you can leave, then plan how you will do it. The better prepared you are, the calmer you can be in yourself. A very violent or aggressive intimate partner may have to be left secretly and then informed afterward. Can you find a shelter for abused women? Can you move to a safe place? I'm aware of the challenge this may be. Use a lawyer if you can; get the help of any kind and understanding person.

I'm suggesting that you leave quickly and in an organized way, just so that it gives you an advantage. Don't be tempted to announce it "to be fair." Narcissists don't know fair play!

One of the things you may see when you look logically at the behavior of a gaslighter who's been spurned is that he or she lives in a world of fantasy. Facts are warped, stories told, and lies rule. This must steel your resolve to heal yourself and will serve as a justification for you playing games with your abuser, which both leaving suddenly and the "gray rock" approach are. You have to protect yourself from abusive, delusional people; don't let anyone try to make you ashamed!

Your reasoning mind and your work to lower your stress, to ground yourself in reality, and overcome the causes of your flashbacks, all mentioned in the previous chapters, are never going to be more necessary than when you resist the person who gaslighted you. It's going to be a struggle, but as I said, it's mostly a battle on the inside, the battle to heal yourself that you started in the very first moment when you realized you'd been gaslighted and that your abuser was - an abuser! So in the face of the list of evil deeds and actions that are possible reactions of a narcissist who's been unmasked and resisted, you have to say to yourself: "I DON'T CARE WHAT THEY SAY! I DON'T CARE WHAT THEY TRY TO DO: I'M NOT TAKING THIS PERSONALLY! I'M NOT LISTENING TO ANY OF IT"; then go ahead and cut off any means of communication such as social media that your gaslighter might use to send you abusive or lying or threatening messages.

 The attack could be open and in the public, or private and secret. It could be both at the same time. Whatever it manifests as, please do not take any of it personally. When other people are used as "flying monkeys," don't lose your temper with them. Give them a reasonable answer if it's called for, but avoid giving information if that's what they've been sent to do.

Really, don't lose your temper in any of this. Too often, losing your temper is thought of as being a successful way to react to aggression - but it's a sign that you've "lost your cool" and that your abuser has power over you. You can be angry - you have a right to be if you've been treated badly - but being angry, and screaming and shouting and insulting back, are not necessarily the same. You can be angry but controlled; seek to be like that.

If you have children with the person who gaslighted you, and you leave, think carefully and caringly about how to handle them. Be calm, and explain what you have to explain to them without being apologetic. Say that you are doing the best thing for everyone. You can mean it! I am painfully aware that most countries and legal systems aren't mindful enough of emotional abuse and narcissism, and that shared custody of children with an abusive character is hardly in the best interests of younger children. I am also concerned by the lack of recognition that a narcissistic, gaslighting mother is not necessarily the automatic choice of parent for any child to live with. I can't ignore the reality of a mother being almost irreplaceable in our earliest years, but male victims with children have a very hard time, on average, deciding when to leave and wanting the best for their child or children. Just persevere with looking after your state of mind: this will help you in your relationship with your children just as much as any other area of your life.

Your abuser may very well play the victim: other people may be presented with tear-jerking, hysterical performances where you are accused of being crazy, unfaithful, and cruel. Narcissists will quite literally accuse their victims of doing whatever they have done to them. This includes calling YOU a narcissist! When other people are taken in - and unfortunately, they often are - you have to be absolutely determined not to let their views change you. Handle them politely and insist that they do not know what you do.

They don't have to see what you saw or suffer what you did. In some cases, other people are co-abusers, such as you may find at work or in a family. If that is the case, you will have to treat them in the same way you treat your principal abuser.

Oh, I nearly forgot... your abuser might try to "love-bomb" you again. If all else fails... The common thread in all the possible reactions is not even apparent abuse, but games, games, and more games. So be clear about that, and do not respond to the "love-bombing" because, as you know all too well, it's not real love in any way. If you do that, you are likely to get the good old abusive reaction back again, i.e., "I invited you, and you just threw my invitation into the trash!!" Answer calmly that an invitation is just that, not a command and that it can be refused, which you prefer to do.

Yes, you've had to deal with a child: a child's rages, sulking, and tantrums, combined with adult knowledge. Your child may even play by putting on a grown-up disdain and appear in public with his or her new "dolly-girl," "toy-boy," "Mommy-Substitute," "Sugar Daddy," or whoever; but it's all a disguise of a childish attitude. Treat it with contempt likewise - the contempt of an adult who really doesn't have to be vindictive and really doesn't need to waste time on childish silliness! If you face danger, be a brave adult, and don't tell yourself that it's better to tolerate being gaslighted because you are facing a challenge. You get nothing from being confused, weakened, and destroyed slowly; nor does anyone else. Abuse has to stop. Sail into the future of recovery and have a fuller, more meaningful life!

I would like you to describe the character of the person who has been gaslighting you. Don't be vindictive, but don't use "sugar-coated" words.

_____

_____

_____

_____

_____

Have you ever left your abuser before or threatened to leave? Or to report a boss or colleague? How did they react?

_____

_____

_____

_____

_____

Put the first two answers together, or look at the first answer if you've never left or threatened to. How do you think your abuser will react when you resist and, or leave them?

_✒_

_____

_____

_____

_____

_____

_____

What practical steps are you going to take to protect and prepare yourself to resist the reaction when you stop accepting being gaslighted when you leave your abuser, if that's possible?

_✒_

_____

_____

_____

_____

_____

_____

Do you see that your abuser is really childish? Describe their childishness.

🖋

_____

_____

_____

_____

_____

_____

What are you going to say to your children, if children are involved, to any other people who are part of your situation, about the choices you have made and the resistance you are putting up?

🖋

_____

_____

_____

_____

_____

_____

CHAPTER 16:

AFFIRMATIONS FOR RESISTING GASLIGHTING

When dealing with overcoming the stored memories and hidden feelings of trauma that a victim experiences with flashbacks, I mentioned having some slogans, mottoes, or catchphrases to help you to focus your mind on reality. These affirmations are to help you not only when you are suffering an emotional flashback; or when your stress levels tell you that you need to relax and put your attention on something positive - but they can be used at any time. Why not repeat some phrase or words in the morning, when waking? When doing an activity to help you to stay healthy, such as jogging? At the end of the day, before you turn out the lights? Or when you want to pray and meditate to, concentrate on the deeper meaning of life, within and above all the things that have happened and are happening to you.

You must have the freedom to think of your own affirmations because your focus and your experience of gaslighting may be quite different from someone else's. However, there are some good ones that others have used, and I will share some with you. You may find them very inspiring and useful.

I'm unique: no one else is the same as me. I don't have to be what my abuser wants me to be.

I don't want "love-bombing"; I need the real thing, and I'm going to start giving it to myself.

He/she doesn't know what love is: I do.

There's real goodness and real love out there – I'm going to persevere to find it by giving it to people who know what real love and goodness are.

I deserve to fulfill my goals!

I'm not going to wallow in guilt — instead, I will learn from my mistakes.

I deserve to have genuine people around me!

I'm going to love people for who they are, not for what I can do for them or get out of them.

People are going to love me for who I am, not for what they can do for me, or get out of me!

I know what I've been through! I'm grounded in reality.

Think of the peace of mind I can enjoy when I stop having to play mind games!

Good people don't use your weaknesses against you: they even help you to overcome them!

I'm not less than my abuser: and he/she isn't more than anyone else. All human beings are equal in worth.

I'm not going to give in! It may be hard, but my life is in God's hands.

Feeling bad isn't an option! It doesn't help anything, so I'm not going to do it.

Today is the first day of the rest of my life!

No, I can't do absolutely everything: I'm only human. Yet I can and will do better than this!

I'm going to turn off the gas lights and let the sunshine in!!

Do I know exactly what's happened? No, but I know I'm being gaslighted!

"But you know that I really love you," your abuser says. "Actually, you don't have a clue what love is. But I do!" you reply.

Yes, my hands were shaking. It was more anger than fear!

The best form of revenge is to start living well!

I have a right to be angry and a duty to let go of it afterward.

You deserve to do this if you enjoy it. When you're happy, you can make other people happy.

I know you (abuser) don't like me being happy, but it makes no difference!

The Emperor has no clothes!

So YOU say I'M the crazy one? Do you know what the word "hypocrite" means? (say to yourself)

If he/she said, "New York's in Germany," I'd just say, "No." If he/she says, "You have to do whatever I say around here," I'll just say, "No."

I don't care that my abuser is using other people to get at me. They're probably hoodwinked, and I know what I've experienced.

My emotions aren't problems – my gaslighting was!

Let yourself realize all the lies and distortions of your abuser; find out the truth!

So you're playing the victim? You're not a very good actor!

– You enjoy hurting other people; I enjoy healing myself.

I don't take any of his/her insults personally: he/she just thinks I'm a chess-piece!

If I'm sensitive, it means I'm aware! That's not a problem: I'm just going to be calm in my awareness.

Yes, it was exhausting. Narcissists are tiring: but once I overcome one, I'll have more energy and experience!

Everything he/she criticizes and insults about me is actually something projected from inside him/her!

God loves me – it's unconditional. I don't have to earn it!

I'm not going to judge a book by its cover – ever again!

I'm going to get to a place of safety: it's my top priority, and I'm not going to be even slightly apologetic about it.

I'm going to give respect, and I'm going to get it back.

I accept myself as I am.

I accept that you are an abuser (say in your mind). It doesn't shock me, scandalize me, or make me afraid anymore. It makes me sad, but I'll get over it.

I don't have to run everything I do past someone else before I do it!

Everywhere I go, I can enjoy calm weather inside my heart.

I have learned from my experiences; I'm stronger now.

"Though the soul's wounds heal, the scars remain. God sees them not as blemishes, but as honors." (Julian of Norwich)

A scar is a sign of healing. I'm not ashamed of my inner scars: they make me more compassionate.

He/she wants me to forgive him/her for dumping his/her rubbish onto me. That's fine: I forgive, but I'm not a dump truck, so he/she will have to find another place to dump the trash next time!

It takes time to heal, but I'm determined to do it completely.

– I am free! Free to create a new and better life. From today...

I'm a country: I have boundaries. I can let people in and welcome them, and I can also keep criminals out. No one has the right to barge into my life and start giving orders.

———— ∞ ————

I was a fool to love too much and to think I could change him/her into another person. But I forgive myself!

———— ∞ ————

I had a past full of hurts: that's why this affected me so much. So it wasn't my fault!

———— ∞ ————

I'm going to be kind to my "inner child" so he/she can grow up in peace and joy!

———— ∞ ————

I was hurt, lonely, and very small. Now I can see myself long ago and love myself, knowing that God is using my 'today' to heal my 'yesterday.'

I can't please everyone all the time!

The things he/she said... I let them go.

If you love someone, you can let them go. If I love myself, I can let go of my past.

You're allowed to say "No" to someone you love!

I can be deeply upset that I was taken advantage of. Crying about it is OK! It's realizing the truth.

I'm going to be healthy: eat well, sleep well, exercise well.

I KNEW something was wrong early on. I forgive myself for not listening.

- Yes, he/she trapped me in "Cloud-Cuckoo Land," but I've found the key to get out!

I long to be loved: let me first love myself, and let God love me; then I can find people to love me.

I can say that I'm capable of love; now let me keep trying in new places!

I'm going to be aware of warning signs in other people – I shall be wary, but not scared! I can protect myself.

I am going to trust my ability to make decisions.

I wasn't in love with you, only with the false feelings you caused in me!

Live in the present: seize the day!

Actually, I have a kind heart. I'm not going to let myself grow cold and cynical!

With goodwill, I can go so far!

The truth of some of the things he/she said doesn't matter because they were said with hate, and hate is abuse.

The truth about myself may hurt, but it heals. I'm going to be healed!

Be brave, and go out there! The world awaits...

Having read these affirmations, what affirmations can you write for yourself?

_____

_____

_____

_____

_____

_____

_____

Which of the affirmations given above, or of your own, are best when you suffer a flashback? Which ones will be useful to say to yourself when or if you have to have some contact with the person who gaslighted you?

_____

_____

_____

_____

_____

_____

_____

Think carefully: when are you going to use affirmations? Plan your day and write which affirmations you will use and when. You need to form some good habits.

_____

_____

_____

_____

_____

_____

_____

_____

At the end of this chapter, I think one of the most important affirmations for a victim of "crazy-making" gaslighting is

"I'M NOT GOING CRAZY!"

CHAPTER 17:

BE STILL, LET GO, AND MOVE AHEAD

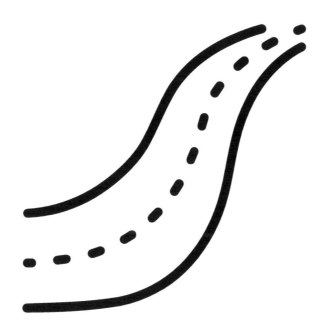

In this workbook, you've been taken through how to recognize manipulation by gaslighting, what exactly was happening to you, and how to resist and recover from it. Now the focus is on your future. You're learning how to be still, let go, and move ahead!

You experienced a lot of stress from a relationship with, or dealing with, a narcissistic type of person; gaslighting was never meant to calm anyone down! Of course, stress is a part of human life – no one is exempt.

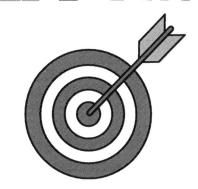

However, you can reduce and handle it so much better using the strategies, techniques, and considerations that I've been guiding you through. You've probably realized that you didn't learn enough of these skills in your childhood and youth, which you needed to have had, but now you can make up for your loss.

Be aware of that "inner critic" and of all the voices in your mind. When I wrote that, I nearly put "in your head" and felt it that sounded bad, as if I were saying you're mad. Of course not! The fact is, as it was pointed out, that our minds run a constant train of thoughts, and those thoughts turn into words. So many people, regrettably, just let these voices, especially the inner critic, drone on and on, at the same time obeying them thoughtlessly. To be truly mindful, you need to check, control, reassure or oppose these little voices. You don't need to silence them - you can't just turn them off instantly - but you need to understand them.

Your reason is not your imagination, and vice versa, and both of them, among others, can produce a mental voice.

The inner voices of your mind, being non-material, move much more quickly than the physical world of your body and your surroundings. This means that we have a tendency to hear a rapid, frenzied train of thoughts when we worry, far quicker than our bodies can work through. All at once, the challenges of each day can come stampeding at us like a herd of frightened cattle: who we have to contact, the cleaning in the house, the decisions to be made, the children's interests, bills to be paid, conflicts to resolve, etcetera, etcetera. No one can tackle these all at once! You need to learn how to be still.

You see, without learning to focus, these types of worries can cause you to have flashbacks, react badly to other people, make mistakes, and/or become physically ill. Ask yourself where they come from - isn't it from your wounded self, your inner child that was traumatized? It's time for you to let go of the past after you've acknowledged it.

Meditation, prayer, mindfulness - any focusing activity - can help you, as I have pointed out before. One important aid to you in being still is to use these methods to focus on the present. Focusing on the present is a way to avoid being enticed into dwelling on the past, regretting it, starting flashbacks. It's also a wonderful way to stop worrying about the future, to stop trying to meet all your challenges at once, when it's only possible to tackle them one by one!

Try this exercise... Find a quiet place to sit down, at the very least where you can be alone. You can do this at home, but you could also do it in a café or a park if you are seated on your own. Breathe slowly, quite deeply, for a while. Then, as you carry on with breathing carefully, concentrate on the present. Only on the present: what can you feel? The seat you're sitting on? The warmth of the sun or the wind? A part of your body that calls your attention? Then ask yourself what you can hear. Is it the traffic? Music from a house nearby? The voices of other people, or the sound of birds chirping and dogs barking? Is the wind blowling? Then, without looking around at anything, in particular, think of what you can see. Where are you? Is the sun shining? Are there other people around you? Can you see the walls of your home? What is in front of you?

Continue breathing carefully and deeply. Now, think of these things you've been focusing on. As they are what you have now. You have a roof over your head or a peaceful park to visit. You have food, drinks and a place to sleep. You know and have known other people, other good people. Be thankful for it all. If food had failed you before, if you hadn't had somewhere to shelter from winter cold and summer heat, you wouldn't be here. You are healthy and have lived to see the world this day. You are a survivor of gaslighting and emotional abuse! You are stronger and happier right now. It's all a gift; we didn't make this world. Yes, it's a difficult and confusing place, but it's also an opportunity. "Today," say to yourself, "is the first day of the rest of my life." Enjoy your 'today.'

After a while, you can let your surroundings come back into focus and carry on living and working. If you feel resistance to stopping a meditation and coming back to your daily life - I know that I do, sometimes - say to yourself that it's because you went through abuse and the problems in your past - and remind yourself that these are dead and gone; you are doing something positive with your life, to fulfill your potential. You're living in the moment: seize the day!

Letting go of the past means embracing the present and being open to the future. The future... while some people lose so much time dreaming about and wanting it, the fact is that often we fear it. We cannot know what it will bring; only make guesses. Are we afraid of it, perhaps, because we think it might be like the past? Remind yourself that you're not helpless; you will learn to meet new challenges just as you've been learning to overcome your recent ones.

You have gifts, talents, and a will to seek the good in life. These things are part of what it means to be human; realize that you have them for a reason and that in them, you will find your motivation. Many victims forget to think of themselves and their goals when they become bonded to an abusive person. This is why they become depressed and feel as if they've stopped living. When you can plan for the future wisely but without paralyzing fear, then you will start to feel much better about it. You will become motivated!

You are worthy of life. Yes, it takes effort to live a full life, and you will have to make an effort to understand, resolve and move on from problems caused by gaslighting of your thoughts by a narcissist or someone at least with this tendency. However, the results are worth it. Our imaginations sometimes make our work difficult by projecting an image of labor so hard that it breaks us. This is a lie and nonsense! Good work is usually done step by step; sometimes, we rest not by doing nothing but by taking part in activities that demand less effort and then returning to more strenuous tasks.

You live from moment to moment, and this is how work is done: by living in the present. Even if 'work' is planning for a future project, you still have to plan by thinking in the present. Don't fear your work. Also, learn to take a break from it. You deserve it.

One of the reasons you fear moving ahead in your life is because your unconscious mind sees all the mess of your life that you've just dealt with, all the things you haven't been able to sort out yet (does anyone really have an empty "In" tray all the time? I don't think so...) and says to you that if life were to carry on like this, it would be awful.

Your unconscious is NOT aware of the future, you see. It cannot project you to your ideals, though it can make calculations on what it remembers of the past. It's very closely tied to your memory.

You have to make it your habit of life to live and work in the present with a desire to plan wisely and positively for the future, using your reason. That's what's going to lift you out of the rut you fell into when you were dependent, or were pushed into by the person or people who gaslighted you. Your unconscious will stop being obsessed with your past failures when you can accept and grieve them, and as you resolve to overcome them; as you're already doing, I hope, as you read this book and do the exercises I've made to guide you through the process.

Think about your "inner critic"; What has this voice been saying to you recently?

_____

_____

_____

_____

_____

_____

What are you afraid of at this point in your life? What really scares you?

_____

_____

_____

_____

_____

_____

_____

So: what are you going to say to yourself to stop your "inner critic" and your fears from spoiling your fun? What can you do to focus on the present and be open to the future with peace?

_____

_____

_____

_____

_____

_____

Try the meditation I gave you in this chapter to focus on the present. When you've done it, write about how you felt afterwards.

_____

_____

_____

_____

_____

_____

_____

Whether you have left the person who gaslighted you or managed to "go no contact, " or even if you have to resist their tactics day by day while you must still live with them... Ask yourself if you can say this in your mind to that abusive person: "I want you to leave me with as much peace as I have from leaving you behind." Even in the latter case where you must still live with your abuser, you've left them mentally and protected yourself inwardly. So: can you let them go?

_____

_____

_____

_____

_____

_____

_____

_____

_____

_____

_____

_____

_____

CONCLUSION

While I was writing this book, my greatest focus was to help a victim of the emotional abuse technique called "gaslighting" to realize that he or she was a victim; and that their abuser was trying to confuse them to control them. This was my greatest concern: have I done that? Because once you, the reader, know you've been gaslighted, that's half the battle won!

You stop trying to explain yourself for the umpteenth time; you stop analyzing yourself and your reactions for the millionth time, to no effect; you stop wondering whether you are in "Cloud-Cuckoo Land," stop wondering why your memory is so bad... What a relief!

In no way do I minimize the damage that emotional abuse can do to your mind and health. Gaslighting ought to be a legally recognized crime. Yet you know, it doesn't matter how badly you've been confused - you can and should and will find the truth. The truth may hurt - yes, that gaslighter doesn't love you, and you haven't seen what they were doing to you; otherwise, you'd have put a stop to it - but the truth heals you. You were in "Cloud-Cuckoo Land," but you found a key to get out, and you did it!

There can be no guarantee that you won't ever come across or start interacting with a gaslighter in the future. Don't stress about that: as a recovering victim, now you are wearing a suit of invisible armor. You know what to look for, how to resist it calmly, and how to protect not only yourself but others. "Once bitten, twice shy." Don't be too scared of meeting new people. When you are assertive, confident, and sensible in your compassion, you are a lot less attractive to a narcissistic type of character. You'll spot them and swat them!

The tools for self-awareness and personal growth I have shared with you are to help you to become the loving, kind and sensitive person you wanted to be but didn't quite know HOW to be. Now you can be all those things, and at the same time, also mature, confident, self-assured, and brave. You can be the woman or the man you were destined to be. Forgive yourself for your mistakes, and live in the present moment, unafraid of the future. Turn out the sickly "gas lights," step out into the real world, and walk forward with your head held high in the bright light of day!

THE LAST EXERCISE

Look at the notes you wrote in the section you drew in the very first exercise, the one that is entitled, "you." What were you feeling then? How were you? Now think of yourself in the present moment and compare who you are, and how you are living your life. what's changed?

Author's Note

Dear reader,
I hope you enjoyed my book.

Please don't forget to toss up a quick review on amazon, I will personally read it! Positive or negative, I'm grateful for all feedback.

Reviews are so helpful for self-published authors and your feedback can make such a difference for my book!

Thanks very much for your time, and I look forward to hearing from you soon.

Sincerely,
Theresa

Made in the USA
Las Vegas, NV
19 November 2024

12155021R00120